MATTHEW ARNOLD
Selected Poems and Prose

THE POETRY BOOKSHELF

General Editor: James Reeves

MATTHEW ARNOLD

MATTHEW ARNOLD

Selected Poems & Prose

Edited with an Introduction and Commentary by

DENYS THOMPSON

BARNES & NOBLE, Inc.

NEW YORK

PUBLISHERS & BOOKSELLERS SINCE 1873

ISBN 389 04076 2

MATTHEW ARNOLD 1822–1888

Introduction and Commentary
© DENYS THOMPSON 1971

First published 1971

First published in the United States by Barnes & Noble,
New York 10003
Printed in Great Britain by Morrison and Gibb Ltd
London and Edinburgh

CONTENTS

NOTE ON THE TEXT

Except for the two youthful works in the Appendix, the poems are in the order in which they were originally published. The text used is that of the 1885 edition, except for poems which did not appear there, and one or two cases where earlier titles have been kept. The prose has been less well served by publishers. There is no complete edition in print, nor will there be till R. H. Super's American volumes (University of Michigan Press, Ann Arbor 1960–) are finished, so the prose extracts here come from miscellaneous sources.

ACKNOWLEDGEMENTS

I am grateful to James Reeves and Anthony Beal for advice, and to Professor Lionel Trilling for helpful information; to the Cambridge University Press for permission to reprint 'Lines Written on the Seashore at Eaglehurst'; and to the Cambridge University Library for the portrait of Arnold from *The Matthew Arnold Birthday Book*, compiled by his daughter Eleanor in 1883.

DENYS THOMPSON

FOREWORD

Arnold's work has affected the lives of many people who have never heard of him; this selection tries to show how this came about. His first response to the currents of thought and action among which he grew up was that of a poet, feeling and writing in the manner of his time. To earn a living he plunged into the wearing and often depressing routine of an inspector of schools, where he looked with penetration on what he found, and then produced the social and literary criticism that has lasted better than the writings of most of his contemporaries and has much to offer to us today.

His life and work, so different in their separate aspects, are presented as a unit of interlocking activities. It is hoped that a fair impression is given of the poet: of the prose writer only a small sample can be presented to show the resources to be tapped in *Culture and Anarchy*, the *Essays in Criticism* and other books that are unfortunately less readily available. Inevitably with an author whose output was fairly copious and certainly varied, it is one reader's Arnold who emerges, but the impression given here can readily be checked by further reading in and about Arnold.

INTRODUCTION

In all his activities Matthew Arnold was concerned with the changes—industrial, social, political—through which he lived. They had started long before his birth on Christmas Eve, 1822, and they were accelerating just before it, when Wellington defeated the French at Waterloo. That victory removed the fear of a foreign power, which for years had made it easy for governments to impose national unity. Restlessness in the country was suppressed by such measures as press censorship, the suspension of Habeas Corpus, the Treasonable Practices Bill and the Combination Act; the culmination was the Peterloo Massacre, when eleven people were killed and many injured in the dispersal of a peaceful crowd by cavalry. In 1822 Castlereagh, the agent of repression, committed suicide—there were cheers at his funeral—and Arnold was born. Political struggles continued throughout his life; the prosperous middle classes sought to wrest power from an aristocracy they saw as hampering their progress, while the lower classes wanted fair treatment and a share in the wealth that their toil had created. Though the mass-meetings that the manual workers held were normally peaceful, Arnold and his contemporaries could not fail to have in mind the French Reign of Terror; before a Chartist demonstration in 1848, government offices were barricaded, guns supplied, and the clerks sworn in as special constables. Arnold's response was different and unapprehensive, for he wanted to get rid of outworn institutions and dogmas, 'the old European system'. Many of the popular demands were met by the Reform Acts, the first of which (in 1832) increased the electorate from under 500,000 to 800,000 by adding middle-class voters. The second, of 1867, gave the vote to rate-paying householders, and by the third the electorate rose in 1883 to about 60 per cent of adult men, though women were still voteless.

Behind the political front were the strains caused by the Industrial Revolution—in essence the replacement of muscle power by steam. At the time of Arnold's birth, the steam-railway system had yet to start, with the opening of the Liverpool–Manchester line in 1830, but as it got going it gave a powerful thrust to the economy. Before his death, however, the invention of the internal-combustion engine—the first Benz car took the road in 1885—signalized the decline of steam and the inception of more far-reaching changes. The Revolution left England a wealthy country, with exports rising from £40 m. a year in 1820 to £230 m. in 1884, and made possible a great increase in the population, which more than doubled in Arnold's lifetime. It also brought misery to millions. The new factories developed the exploitation of women and children, who already worked like slaves in the mines. At the time of the Great Exhibition of 1851 the Prince Consort said, in the official catalogue:

> The first impression which the view of this vast collection will produce will be that of deep thankfulness to the Almighty for the blessings which he has bestowed upon us already here below; and the second, the conviction that they can be only realized in proportion to the help which we are prepared to render to each other—therefore, only by peace, love, and ready assistance, not only between individuals, but between the nations of the earth.

To this happy state child-labour made a substantial contribution, for in the same year there were in industrial employment 1,205 children aged five, 203,300 aged fourteen, and in all about 600,000 of up to fourteen. Employment did at least prevent starvation, which was sometimes the lot of those who were not employed. Demobilization after Waterloo threw 300,000 men onto the labour market; in the years 1837–1842, when there was a run of bad harvests, 'conditions for the mass of the British people were worse than ever since, and in certain respects than ever before' (Derek Beales); and in 1866–1867 more bad harvests caused intense distress, the workhouses were full and men fought for work. Rural conditions were little better, especially after the start of the so-called Great Depression of 1873 onwards.

As people flocked from the villages to the towns, so the towns swelled, with ready-made slums for the factory workers flung up as cheaply as possible, without sewerage, adequate water or public services. The Chadwick Sanitary Report of 1842 revealed conditions in London that were paralleled in the wretched towns of the North and Midlands, conditions vividly described by Dickens in *Hard Times*, and on a larger and more sharply focused canvas in Henry Mayhew's *London Labour and the London Poor*, a careful and deeply impressive document. Such was the setting of Arnold's thirty-five years as an inspector of elementary schools.

Matthew was six years old when his father, the Rev. Thomas Arnold, who hitherto had made a living by tutoring young men, was appointed Headmaster of Rugby School. This he set about reforming, so vigorously and effectively that he influenced not only other decayed boarding schools but the majority of boys' secondary schools almost up to the present day. He sent Matthew to his old school, Winchester College—where the young Arnold did not win popularity by telling the headmaster that he found the work easy—and then after a year to his own school at Rugby. Before he was fourteen Matthew wrote the first poem of his that has survived (see the Appendix), and at Rugby won a prize for poetry. Thence he gained a scholarship to Balliol College, Oxford, where he did little work and affected fancy waistcoats, an elaborate hair-style and a dilettante irresponsibility. An example of this occurred on a coach trip to Devon with a friend, who afterwards revealed that 'Our friend Matt . . . pleasantly induced a belief into the passengers of the coach that I was a poor mad gentleman, and that he was my keeper'.

3

After Oxford—his father had died during his time there—Arnold taught for a short time at Rugby. In 1845 he was awarded a fellowship by Oriel College, Oxford, though he did not take up the academic life. When he was twenty-five he fell deeply in love with 'Marguerite', a French girl whom he met in Switzerland, but the affair ended in unhappiness for Arnold. As Secretary for a short time to Lord Lansdowne, President of the Council, he gained first-hand knowledge of the ruling aristocracy, the 'Barbarians' whose unfitness for government he later deplored in *Culture and Anarchy*. Then in 1849 he published anonymously his first book, *The Strayed Reveller and Other Poems* (of which 'Shakespeare' and 'The Forsaken Merman' are included here). It had some rather trifling reviews, and Arnold soon withdrew the book. It did however make a considerable impact on his friends and relatives, who realized for the first time that Arnold was in fact a most serious person. His sister Mary, writing to another sister, wrote: 'These poems have made me . . . know him better than I ever did before and expect much more from him—they have given me as it were a look into his mind . . .' It was in September of this year, 1849, that Arnold himself wrote to his friend, Arthur Hugh Clough:

> These are damned times—everything is against one—the height to which knowledge is come, the spread of luxury, our physical enervation, the absence of great *natures*, the unavoidable contact with millions of small ones, cities, light profligate friends, moral desperadoes like Carlyle, our own selves, and the sickening consciousness of our difficulties.

Another set of changes, in which Arnold was closely involved, led to the establishment of a complete national system of elementary schools. The first state grants for education had been made in 1833, and six years later the Committee of Council on Education was formed. It was to this body that Arnold was responsible when at the age of twenty-eight he was appointed Her Majesty's Inspector of Schools, through Lord Lansdowne's influence. He sought the post to get a salaried position, for his future father-in-law was not enthusiastic about his daughter's marrying an elegant but penniless young poet, and as soon as he was appointed he married Frances Lucy Wightman. His district at first was enormous (though as he continued in the government service it was steadily reduced) and involved a great deal of wearisome travel. Naturally he disliked this part of it, and the very trying conditions under which he often had to work, and he never disguised the fact from his wife and friends; but the work itself soon absorbed him. Even in his first year, 1851, he wrote to his wife:

I think I shall get interested in the schools after a little time; their effects on the children are so immense, and their future effects in civilizing the next generation of the lower classes, who, as things are going, will have most of the political power of the country in their hands, may be so important.

This is no more the writing of a man who is doing a despised job for money than are the wise and perceptive reports that he soon started to produce. In one of his earliest he favoured co-education and recommended the provision of infant schools. He was an efficient and respected official, kindly towards children, considerate and helpful to teachers; he would encourage any likely ones to gain further qualification. His work took him through some of the worst slums that have existed, where schools could be very unpleasant places; one observer speaks of the children of 'the wild nomadic hordes that throng through the manufacturing cities'. There is abundant testimony to his charm and effectiveness from teachers and others, and even if this evidence did not exist, his reports and other educational writings show the quality of the mind and concern that he brought to his work. The reports were courageous and out-spoken. He bitterly criticized the Revised Code adopted by his superiors for elementary schools both before and after it took effect; it would be disastrous, he urged, in the damage it inflicted

5

on education by its system of payment by results and by the very narrow 'practical' curriculum that it imposed. After the Code had been in operation for ten years he wrote:

> The whole use that the Government makes of the mighty engine of literature in the education of the working classes amounts to little more, even when most successful, than in giving them the power to read the newspapers.

It is sad that Arnold's intervention was unsuccessful, and that this curriculum directive was not abandoned till after his death. On one occasion a particularly outspoken report was sent back to Arnold to revise; he refused to revise it. Again, in 1864, his superiors would not publish a report of his, and it was suppressed. No civil servant has ever so directly and so publicly opposed a policy he was obliged to carry out as a duty. In such a case he wrote to his wife: 'I don't think . . . they can eject me, though they can and perhaps will, make my place uncomfortable. If thrown on the world I dare say we should be on our legs again before very long.'

However it must be said for his superiors that they recognized his extraordinary value, and duly promoted him. Moreover the wearisome routine of inspecting was lightened on three occasions when, with his good knowledge of French, he was sent to study educational systems on the Continent—visits which supplied the material for books of lasting importance as well as for official reports. He also made a lecture tour of the United States, which he enjoyed, though he found the segregation of children in the state schools depressing, and was very badly treated by the newspapers. Another event that gave him pleasure was his appointment as (non-resident) Professor of Poetry at Oxford, a post which he held for ten years.

His life was saddened by the death of three of his four sons before they reached adulthood. He retired from his official post in 1886, but lived only for another eighteen months. He had gone to Liverpool to meet his much-loved elder daughter on her return from America; in a moment of haste he ran, tripped and died.

After the first anonymous book of poems he published others in 1852, 1853 and 1855, a poetic drama, 'Merope', and in 1867 *New Poems*, a volume which in fact contained a number that had already been published. To the present-day reader of his poetry three questions present themselves: the relationship of his verse to his critical and educational writing; his standing in comparison with other poets of the century; and his ceasing to write poetry in the last thirty years of his life.

Arnold wrote much about the nature of poetry, the assessment of its merit, and the function it may perform, especially in education. His views are summed up in a paragraph early in his essay on Maurice de Guérin, which starts with the words:

> The grand power of poetry is its interpretative power; by which I mean, not a power of drawing out in black and white an explanation of the mystery of the universe, but the power of so dealing with things as to awaken in us a wonderfully full, new, and intimate sense of them, and of our relations with them.

In addition he wanted poetry to be consoling and bracing, and to induce a capacity for action; in short, to be 'adequate' to the time in which it is written—the word he used in his Inaugural Lecture at Oxford. 'It must guide the idea-moved masses; it must clarify their ideas. It must quiet and compose them. It must be fortifying.'

There are certainly signs in his poetry that Arnold aspired to this adequacy, mainly in the form of asides and comments and a gentle dissatisfaction. He often refers to modern life, especially the life of cities, as in 'Lines Written in Kensington Gardens' and near the close of 'Thyrsis'. In the cities of a 'sick age', characterized by a 'harsh, heart-wearying roar', 'most men in a brazen prison live'; and in a poem 'Consolation' (not included here) he wrote:

> A vague depression
> Weighs down my soul.

Of course many such expressions are spoken in character, and isolated examples may not be a fair reflection of Arnold's attitude. But instances could be multiplied, and they combine to give us an impression of the poet's outlook:

> on this iron time
> Of doubts, disputes, distractions, fears

and on

> this strange disease of modern life
> With its sick hurry, its divided aims.

After this sad, resigned lament over an age he found hostile, with longing glances by contrast to other ages and other scenes, the poet's response seems to be withdrawal. This is the theme of both 'Thyrsis' and 'The Scholar Gipsy', who is bidden to 'Fly our feverish contact', and it appears to be implicit in the first of his poems to succeed in its way, 'The Forsaken Merman', as well as in his finest and late poem, 'Dover Beach'. On the other hand there is sometimes a rather forced resolve, as in 'Rugby Chapel'. After asking, and replying for the majority:

> What is the course of the life
> Of mortal men on the earth?
> Most men eddy about . . .

he goes on to describe those who are different, and the somewhat grim attitude they adopt:

> With frowning foreheads, with lips
> Sternly compressed, we strain on . . .

Among other Victorian poets, this reminds us of W. E. Henley's would-be heroic stance:

> Out of the night that covers me,
>   Black as the pit from pole to pole,
> I thank whatever gods may be
>   For my unconquerable soul . . .

rather than of Hopkins'

> O the mind, mind has mountains; cliffs of fall
> Frightful, sheer, no-man-fathomed.

Hopkins, a Jesuit priest, exactly contemporary with Arnold, gives a clear impression in his poetry of a man who has apprehended reality; whereas Arnold, more gifted and more sympathetic to the modern reader than most poets of the age, leading an active life of travel and valuable work, wrote most of his poetry before he was thirty-five, and had virtually ceased by forty-five, as if poetry was not a voice through which he could speak in his maturity.

Despite the beauty and appeal of his verse he leaves us with the impression that he glanced at the violently changing world and shrank away from it. It is not as if his poetry was written as a by-product; he intensely wanted to be taken seriously as a poet, and thought that he would eventually be judged Tennyson's superior, as having more intellectual weight. But his strength lay elsewhere. Despite the quality of his critical writing—he wrote more fully and more profitably about poetry than any other Victorian—he was completely a poet of his time, sharing with his contemporaries a partial view of poetry that came to them through their being overshadowed by the great Romantics, such as Wordworth and Keats, and by Milton before them. The bent of the Victorians was to take from other poets what fitted their need, and at various times they adopted, for example, the mere sonority of Milton, his similes (as in 'Sohrab and Rustum'), the surface of Keats' style, and what they took to be Wordsworth's style and outlook. Such influences can be seen throughout Arnold's poetry, from the juvenile poem printed in the Appendix, with its echoes of Milton and Gray, to the Keatsian effects in much of 'Thyrsis' and 'The Scholar Gipsy'.

With some remarkable exceptions, Arnold was also a Victorian when it came to 'placing' poets. In exalting his great predecessors he found no room for those who did not readily fit the poetic preconceptions of his age. For instance, in 'The Study of Poetry' he examines the work of Dryden and Pope, and concludes:

> It is the poetry of the builders of an age of prose and reason. Though they may write in verse, though they may in a certain sense be masters of the art of versification, Dryden and Pope are not classics of our poetry, they are classics of our prose.

The range of topics and treatment permitted to poets is thus restricted, and satire, wit, irony cannot be poetic. It is not surprising, then, that Arnold includes in his list of the chief poets of three hundred years Gray, Goldsmith, Cowper, Walter Scott, Burns and Campbell, but finds no place for Dunbar, Donne and the Metaphysical poets, Marvell, Blake or Christopher Smart.

Thus his poetry is limited with few exceptions to 'pleasant' subjects, and the moods tend to be of longing, regret and reflection. Within these limits his successes are memorable, like that of 'The Forsaken Merman'; once read, preferably aloud, its plangent tones are not quickly forgotten. It seems, incidentally, to be the Victorian poem that most often appeals to teenagers. In 'Sohrab and Rustum' the pictorial similes decorate a set piece that really comes to life in the felt description of the contest between father and son—'felt', in the judgement of many readers, because this part of the poem symbolizes the relationship between Arnold and his own powerful father. He excels at evoking the beauty of the mid-nineteenth century rural landscape, when as a result of planned tree-planting and careful cultivation the English countryside was at its pitch of loveliness, providing an environment that was visually one of the most satisfying evolved by man. The humanized landscape is almost as much the theme of the two elegies as it is of the 'Lines Written in Kensington Gardens'. For it is lines such as these that draw readers to return to them with pleasure:

> Where is the girl, who by the boatman's door,
>   Above the locks, above the boating throng,
>   Unmoored our skiff when through the Wytham flats,

Red loosestrife and blond meadow-sweet among
And darting swallows and light water-gnats,
　　We tracked the shy Thames shore?
Where are the mowers, who, as the tiny swell
Of our boat passing heaved the river-grass,
　　Stood with suspended scythe to see us pass?
They all are gone, and thou art gone as well!

For modern readers Arnold has gained incidental strength from the destruction in an overcrowded island of the countryside in which he set his elegies.

In some of his poems the natural scene is an almost indulgently sought refuge. This is not so in 'Dover Beach'. The tranquillity of the scene is admirably conveyed in the calm movement of the opening lines. The sea, the sight and sound of it beautifully presented, is an element of the poem's being, not, like the earlier 'Homeric' similes, a decoration; and the reader receives the impression on his senses before he understands the poetry intellectually. What the sound of the waves once meant to Sophocles leads into the heart of the poem, the ebbing of the sea of faith, the loss of which, poignantly felt here, was the predicament of Arnold's time. In the conclusion he returns to his companion, expressing his belief that human beings must rely on their being true to each other in tragic acceptance of their plight. More than any other poem of his, 'Dover Beach' meets the demand made in the Oxford inaugural lecture that modern poetry must be adequate to its time.

Lionel Trilling and other writers believe that his work as an inspector of schools hastened the end of Arnold as a poet, and W. H. Auden, in his short poem 'Matthew Arnold' (in *Another Time*), seems to agree that the best in him was thwarted:

　　. . . 'I am my father's forum and he shall be heard,
　　Nothing shall contradict his holy final word,
　　Nothing.' And thrust his gift in prison till it died,

And left him nothing but a jailor's voice and face,
And all rang hollow but the clear denunciation
Of a gregarious optimistic generation
That saw itself already in a father's place.

It depends on the view one takes of Arnold's 'gift'. In different conditions he might have gone on to write more poetry, but there is no strong hint in the poetry that he did write that had he written more the poems would have been of a different kind and quality. In turning to write on literature, society and education he became one of the nineteenth century's most influential figures, much more highly regarded today than most of his contemporaries. Though it can be said that his prose superseded his poetry, it would be truer to say with Professor Trilling that 'the poet's vision gave the prose writer his goal' and that Arnold the poet first felt the problems that Arnold the 'practical' man endeavoured to solve.

Arnold, as we have noted, looked for adequacy to its age in good poetry. This was an early statement, and he was to develop it in his later writing, notably in his essay on Wordsworth, in which occurs the well-known dictum that poetry is 'a criticism of life'—and not only poetry but all good literature, as he makes clear elsewhere. 'How to live', Arnold says, is one of the most important questions a man has to answer. The best poems are truthful and serious and we can see in them the application of ideas to life, to the question of how to live. 'Criticism' in Arnold's sense means, not carping, but seeing clearly, understanding and interpreting to others. When he urged that 'most of what passes with us for religion and philosophy will be replaced by poetry' he went further than most readers would follow, though we may well agree that Arnold's strength lies 'in his awareness that poetry has its roots in a kind of wisdom . . . and its effect in the animation of the reader for the daily business of living' (Vincent Buckley).

The poetry that is adequate to its task of being a criticism of life must have the truth and seriousness that we should now term 'sincerity', in the deepest meaning we can give to it. This quality of excellence is manifest in style: 'The superior character of truth and seriousness, in the matter and substance of the best poetry, is inseparable from the superiority of diction and movement marking its style and manner'. In order to know 'the truly excellent' when we meet it we must have developed the power of recognition by becoming acquainted with the best literature, and bring our recollection and experience of it to bear when making up our minds about something new. If we are 'thoroughly penetrated' by the power of good poetry, we carry with us a notion of its excellence in the form of the 'touchstones' of which Arnold provides examples in 'The Study of Poetry'. The touchstones were not portable scales, as his own practice makes clear—in his analysis in the first lecture on translating Homer of various versions, and near the end of 'The Study of Poetry' in his acute and generous appreciation of Burns.

Arnold himself observed that 'whoever seriously occupies himself with literature will soon perceive its vital connection with other agencies'—a remark that fully applied to its writer. Every one of his activities related to the others. He started life as a poet; he earned his living by being (what he soon became) an expert on education; and he first made a name for himself as a critic who brought out the relationship between literature and life. It was as a literary critic that he wrote the paragraph on the need for change in the essay on Heine quoted on p. 114. What he wanted his readers to see in particular was that the lives and actions of so many people who mattered were unsatisfactory. The masses were brutalized by the urban conditions created by the Industrial Revolution; the middle classes accepted it all so long as it brought them material progress; the ruling aristocracy was effete and futile. This view he first expressed in the essay on 'Democracy', part of which is included here, and later enlarged in *Culture and Anarchy*, where he dubbed the three classes Barbarians, Philistines, Populace. The Barbarians, who governed, were unfit to do so, and there was no prospect of their improving—they were incapable of understanding what was happening. The Philistines (the middle class) present 'a defective type of religion, a narrow range of intellect and knowledge, a stunted sense of beauty, a low standard of manners' (Notebooks, p. 542). Arnold's hope was that the middle classes, of whose virtues he spoke elsewhere, would educate themselves to replace the ruling aristocracy, and then to educate the lower classes, the Populace, to exercise responsibly the political power that was coming to them. As things were, some of the Populace became Barbarians, and came to share their outlook and lack of ideals; the remainder 'raw and half-developed, has long lain half-hidden amidst its poverty and squalor, and is now issuing from its hiding-place to assert an Englishman's heaven-born privilege of doing as he likes . . .'

Later in his life, however, Arnold must have felt some disappointment with his efforts for the education of the middle classes, because for nearly ten years, from 1870, he turned directly to the working classes. He addressed them in a series of religious works that included *Literature and Dogma*, *God and the Bible* and *Last Essays on Church and Religion*, the character of which was more overtly moral and less intellectual than that of his other books. He wanted the masses to be influenced by religion, not the materialistic religion of the day, but one transformed. In explaining his view of what the transformation should be he seems to see religion as meeting deep human needs:

> The power of Christianity has been in the immense emotion which it has excited; in its engaging, for the government of man's conduct, the mighty forces of love, reverence, gratitude, hope, pity, and awe —all that host of allies which Wordsworth included under the one name of *imagination* . . .—*God and the Bible*

Whether these religious writings reached the readers for whom they were intended has been doubted. Beyond doubt, however, are the clear results of his thought and work for education. He showed uncommon farsightedness in campaigning ceaselessly for a complete educational system to be provided by the State, first at the elementary level and then at the secondary stage; administration should be local, to avoid the dangers of a centralized bureaucracy. It was important, he contended, that the State should offer secondary education, so that the middle classes could be prepared for their task of training others—for in Arnold's time they had no choice between the ancient and decayed boarding-schools of the Barbarians and the wretched swindles of the kind exposed by Dickens in *Nicholas Nickleby* (see the end of Chapter III). Arnold incidentally envisaged the fitting of the public schools into the State system. Good secondary education would transform the middle classes and enable them to civilize the masses, degraded by their working and living conditions. This comprehensive view was based on first-hand knowledge. Arnold had attended two boarding-schools and had taught at one of them, and he knew what they produced. His thorough investigation of Continental education made it clear to him what was lacking in England at the secondary stage. As an inspector he was in close daily contact with elementary schools, their environment, and their pupils, staff and managers.

Thus he had a clear picture of the needs. First he vigorously rejected the middle-class idea that schooling for the masses should be the provision of purely vocational education at the cheapest possible rate, solely to maintain the supply of competent workers in office and factory. This prompted Arnold's strenuous opposition to the Revised Code of instruction for elementary schools and later to proposals for exclusively technical education for the lower and middle classes. This was the negative side of his setting out the large task he envisaged for the schools. In his analysis, the changes of his time, unless intelligently managed—we must not be 'acrid solvents', as he wrote in his 'Heine' essay—would involve social and cultural disruption. He looked for the springs of political progress and change in the mind of the people—'the fermenting mind of the nation'. But this mind had to be educated, and this led him to lay constant emphasis, which can be seen even in the brief selection from his reports included here, on the humanizing function of the schools: 'The State has an interest in the primary school as a *civilizing* agent, even prior to its interest in it as an instructing agent.'

The means of this humanizing was to be found in literature: 'what is comprised under the word literature is in itself the greatest power available in education; of this power it is not too much to say that in our elementary schools at present no use is made at all.' The power was at its strongest in poetry:

> Good poetry does undoubtedly tend to form the soul and character; it tends to beget a love of beauty and truth in alliance together, it suggests, however indirectly, high and noble principles of action, and it inspires the emotion so helpful in making principles operative. Hence its extreme importance to all of us; but in our elementary schools its importance seems to me to be at present quite extraordinary.—*Report of 1880*

Arnold was emphatic because he saw that schools under the Revised Code were able to provide only a narrow course of arithmetic and 'English', and did nothing for the emotional growth of their pupils. He looked for all-round development, and despite a good-natured controversy with his friend T. H. Huxley over the relationship between science and literature in education, he upheld the liberalizing power of science as well as that of letters. Though Arnold himself was fond of fishing and of strenuous exercise like swimming, he attached little importance to organized games in school—the Barbarians excelled at them. Again, however important literature was, 'It cannot do all. In other words literature is a part of civilization; it is not the whole' (Preface to *Mixed Essays*). He summed up his beliefs in the essay on 'Sweetness and Light', part of which is reproduced in these pages.

As a poet Arnold is read for a handful of good poems. They

come from one of the best minds of the time; they give pleasure without surprise or shock. The poetic preconceptions of his time restricted his range, and the mild civilized discontent that pervades his verse contrasts sharply with the clarity and vigour of his prose. As a literary critic he made a strong case for poetry at a time when Utilitarian views would have pushed it out of education as irrelevant, and when Charles Darwin in his later years wrote so movingly:

> If I had to live my life over again, I would have made a rule to read some poetry and listen to some music at least once every week; for perhaps the parts of my brain now atrophied would thus have been kept active through use. The loss of these tastes is a loss of happiness, and may possibly be injurious to the intellect, and more probably to the moral character, by enfeebling the emotional part of our nature.
> —*Autobiography*

In the practice of criticism his perceptions transcended the limitations of his time, when he saw the strength of Keats and the value of Burns. As a writer on the society in which he lived his analysis gained wide and lasting assent, even if there has been neglect of his view that what matters in the solving of problems is the quality of mind brought to bear on them. When Arnold's contemporary, Frederic Harrison, criticized culture as simply 'a turn for small-fault-finding, love of selfish ease, and indecision in action' he forgot that everything Arnold said was grounded in his daily work, forgot that the advocate of culture knew the circumstances, saw the need, and supplied practical recommendations, all with decisiveness, steady application, and courage. It is natural that one who set himself high standards and upheld them consistently should meet with opposition, then and now. One charge against him is that he made resounding and impressive statements, and left it at that without providing close argument. There is weight in it: he was a Victorian; he could use such phrases as 'reason and the will of God' with a confidence now impossible; and other statements strike the reader of today as claiming too much or in need of re-casting in the light of current knowledge. Again, Raymond Williams makes the fair point that Arnold shrank from 'extending his criticism of ideas to criticism of the social and economic system from which they proceeded'. This is a limitation, one feels, that is due to his frame of mind; he gives the impression of having left economics to other people. But it has not stopped later critics of the socio-economic system from finding an ally in Arnold. Again it has been noted several times that there is a contradiction between his genuine concern for equality and his belief, expressed after a condemnation of the Barbarians, Philistines and Populace as such, that within each class there are some people who are led not by the class spirit but by the love of human perfection. In all these aspects the limitations apparent are those of his period, and against them must be set the directions in which he escaped them. One need only compare Arnold with the other protestors of the Victorian era—Carlyle, Ruskin, Newman, to say nothing of Pater, Morris and Wilde—to see where the superiority lies.

Arnold's influence has been wide and lasting. In writing on the relation between literature and life, critics such as I. A. Richards and F. R. Leavis started from Arnold's position, though they diverged after that. Writers on society who have been deeply affected by Arnold include R. H. Tawney and Raymond Williams. In education above all he has been the source of many ideas, first and directly in the elementary, now primary, schools. The headmaster of one of them, George Sampson, wrote: 'Matthew Arnold's enduring freshness is due in part, at least, to his humanizing contact with children and his sympathy with them.' On secondary schools he has been a powerful influence through the numbers of teachers, administrators and writers on education whose minds he has helped to make up. Negatively this influence is due to his having left matters of classroom technique to teachers; he was never too much concerned with what might be ephemeral. Positively, he has prompted in many a commitment to education, while his principles have worked for the bringing-up of children as growing human beings, not vessels to be filled or hands to be trained for factory, ballot-box, or the acquiring of consumer goods.

For what he saw amiss in Victorian England he had no panacea, his insistent habit being to ask the right questions. If we attempt the answers for our own times, it will be worth considering part of Raymond Williams's summing-up:

> We shall, if we are wise, continue to listen to him, and, when the time comes to reply, we can hardly speak better than in his own best spirit. For if we centre our attention on a tradition of thinking rather than on an isolated man, we shall not be disposed to underrate what he did and what he represented, or to neglect what he urged us, following him, to do.—*Culture and Society 1780–1950*, p. 136.

SUGGESTIONS FOR FURTHER READING

1. ARNOLD'S WORKS

Poetical Works, edited by C. B. Tinker and H. F. Lowry (Oxford
University Press 1950)
    The most convenient edition, with full textual notes showing how
Arnold altered his poems.

The Poems of Matthew Arnold, edited by Kenneth Allott (Longmans
1965)
    This contains a few more poems, and is very thoroughly annotated.

Matthew Arnold and the New Order, edited by Peter Smith and Geoffrey
Summerfield (Cambridge University Press 1969)
    Two important essays, otherwise inaccessible, with a good selection
from the Reports, an excellent introduction and detailed notes.

Essays in Criticism, First Series, with introduction by G. K. Chesterton
(Dent 1906)

Essays in Criticism, Second Series, edited by S. R. Littlewood (Macmillan
1938)

Culture and Anarchy, edited by J. Dover Wilson (Cambridge University
Press 1932)

The Essential Matthew Arnold (Chatto and Windus 1969), edited by
Lionel Trilling, contains verse and prose, including a number of
Arnold's letters.

2. ARNOLD AND HIS TIMES

Derek Beales, *From Castlereagh to Gladstone, 1815-1885* (Nelson 1969)

Vincent Buckley, *Poetry and Morality* (Chatto and Windus 1959)

W. F. Connell, *The Educational Thought and Influence of Matthew Arnold*
(Routledge 1950)

J. D. Jump, *Matthew Arnold* (Longmans 1955)

F. R. Leavis, *The Common Pursuit* (Chatto and Windus 1952; Penguin
Books 1962)

Henry Mayhew, *London Street Life*, edited by R. O'Malley (Chatto and Windus 1966)

Fred G. Walcott, *The Origins of Culture and Anarchy* (Heinemann Educational Books 1970)

R. J. White, *Waterloo to Peterloo* (Heinemann 1957; Penguin Books 1968)

Raymond Williams, *Culture and Society 1780–1950* (Chatto and Windus 1958; Penguin Books 1961)

PART ONE

Poems

Shakespeare

OTHERS abide our question. Thou art free.
We ask and ask: Thou smilest and art still,
Out-topping knowledge. For the loftiest hill
That to the stars uncrowns his majesty,
Planting his steadfast footsteps in the sea,
Making the Heaven of Heavens his dwelling-place,
Spares but the cloudy border of his base
To the foil'd searching of mortality:
And thou, who didst the stars and sunbeams know,
Self-school'd, self-scann'd, self-honour'd, self-secure,   10
Didst walk on Earth unguess'd at. Better so!
All pains the immortal spirit must endure,
    All weakness that impairs, all griefs that bow,
    Find their sole voice in that victorious brow.

The Forsaken Merman

COME, dear children, let us away;
Down and away below!
Now my brothers call from the bay;
Now the great winds shoreward blow;
Now the salt tides seaward flow;
Now the wild white horses play,

Champ and chafe and toss in the spray.
Children dear, let us away!
This way, this way!

Call her once before you go—
Call once yet!
In a voice that she will know:
'Margaret! Margaret!'
Children's voices should be dear
(Call once more) to a mother's ear:
Children's voices, wild with pain.
Surely she will come again!
Call her once and come away.
This way, this way!
'Mother dear, we cannot stay.'
The wild white horses foam and fret.
Margaret! Margaret!

Come, dear children, come away down.
Call no more!
One last look at the white-wall'd town,
And the little grey church on the windy shore.
Then come down!
She will not come though you call all day.
Come away, come away!

    Children dear, was it yesterday
We heard the sweet bells over the bay?
In the caverns where we lay,
Through the surf and through the swell,
The far-off sound of a silver bell?
Sand-strewn caverns, cool and deep,
Where the winds are all asleep;
Where the spent lights quiver and gleam;
Where the salt weed sways in the stream;

10

20

30

Where the sea-beasts, rang'd all round,
Feed in the ooze of their pasture-ground;
Where the sea-snakes coil and twine,
Dry their mail and bask in the brine;
Where great whales come sailing by,
Sail and sail, with unshut eye,
Round the world for ever and aye?
When did music come this way?
Children dear, was it yesterday?

Children dear, was it yesterday
(Call yet once) that she went away?
Once she sate with you and me,
On a red gold throne in the heart of the sea,
And the youngest sate on her knee.
She comb'd its bright hair, and she tended it well,
When down swung the sound of a far-off bell.
She sigh'd, she look'd up through the clear green sea.
She said; 'I must go, for my kinsfolk pray
In the little grey church on the shore to-day.
'Twill be Easter-time in the world—ah me!
And I lose my poor soul, Merman, here with thee!
I said; 'Go up, dear heart, through the waves;
Say thy prayer, and come back to the kind sea-caves.'
She smil'd, she went up through the surf in the bay.
Children dear, was it yesterday?

  Children dear, were we long alone?
'The sea grows stormy, the little ones moan.
Long prayers,' I said, 'in the world they say.
Come,' I said, and we rose through the surf in the bay.
We went up the beach, by the sandy down
Where the sea-stocks bloom, to the white-wall'd town.
Through the narrow pav'd streets, where all was still,

27

To the little grey church on the windy hill.
From the church came a murmur of folk at their prayers,
But we stood without in the cold blowing airs.
We climb'd on the graves, on the stones worn with rains,
And we gaz'd up the aisle through the small leaded panes.
She sate by the pillar; we saw her clear:
'Margaret, hist! come quick, we are here!
Dear heart,' I said, 'we are long alone.
The sea grows stormy, the little ones moan.'
But, ah, she gave me never a look,   80
For her eyes were seal'd to the holy book!
Loud prays the priest; shut stands the door.
Come away, children, call no more!
Come away, come down, call no more!

   Down, down, down!
Down to the depths of the sea!
She sits at her wheel in the humming town,
Singing most joyfully.
Hark, what she sings; 'O joy, O joy,
For the humming street, and the child with its toy!   90
For the priest, and the bell, and the holy well.
For the wheel where I spun,
And the blessed light of the sun.'
And so she sings her fill,
Singing most joyfully,
Till the spindle drops from her hand,
And the whizzing wheel stands still.
She steals to the window, and looks at the sand;
And over the sand at the sea;
And her eyes are set in a stare;   100
And anon there breaks a sigh,
And anon there drops a tear,
From a sorrow-clouded eye,
And a heart sorrow-laden,

28

A long, long sigh,
For the cold strange eyes of a little Mermaiden,
And the gleam of her golden hair.

   Come away, away children.
Come children, come down!
The hoarse wind blows colder;   110
Lights shine in the town.
She will start from her slumber
When gusts shake the door;
She will hear the winds howling,
Will hear the waves roar.
We shall see, while above us
The waves roar and whirl,
A ceiling of amber,
A pavement of pearl.
Singing, 'Here came a mortal,   120
But faithless was she!
And alone dwell for ever
The kings of the sea.'

But, children, at midnight,
When soft the winds blow;
When clear falls the moonlight;
When spring-tides are low:
When sweet airs come seaward
From heaths starr'd with broom;
And high rocks throw mildly   130
On the blanch'd sands a gloom:
Up the still, glistening beaches,
Up the creeks we will hie;
Over banks of bright seaweed
The ebb-tide leaves dry.
We will gaze, from the sand-hills,

At the white, sleeping town;
At the church on the hill-side—
  And then come back down.
Singing, 'There dwells a lov'd one,   140
But cruel is she!
She left lonely for ever
The kings of the sea.'

POEMS FROM THE 1852 VOLUME

Cadmus and Harmonia

FROM *Empedocles on Etna*

To the banished Empedocles in a 'fierce, man-hating mood' the young
harp-player, Callicles, sings these words:

        Far, far from here,
    The Adriatic breaks in a warm bay
    Among the green Illyrian hills; and there
    The sunshine in the happy glens is fair,
    And by the sea, and in the brakes.
    The grass is cool, the sea-side air
    Buoyant and fresh, the mountain flowers
    As virginal and sweet as ours.
    And there, they say, two bright and aged snakes,
    Who once were Cadmus and Harmonia,   10
    Bask in the glens or on the warm sea-shore,
    In breathless quiet, after all their ills.
    Nor do they see their country, nor the place
    Where the Sphinx lived among the frowning hills,
    Nor the unhappy palace of their race,
    Nor Thebes, nor the Ismenus, any more.

There those two live, far in the Illyrian brakes.
They had stay'd long enough to see,
In Thebes, the billow of calamity
Over their own dear children roll'd,   20
Curse upon curse, pang upon pang,
For years, they sitting helpless in their home,
A grey old man and woman; yet of old
The Gods had to their marriage come,
And at the banquet all the Muses sang.

Therefore they did not end their days
In sight of blood; but were rapt, far away,
To where the west wind plays,
And murmurs of the Adriatic come
To those untrodden mountain lawns; and there   30
Placed safely in changed forms, the Pair
Wholly forget their first sad life, and home,
And all that Theban woe, and stray
For ever through the glens, placid and dumb. . . .

Absence

IN this fair stranger's eyes of grey
Thine eyes, my love, I see.
I shudder: for the passing day
Had borne me far from thee.

This is the curse of life: that not
A nobler calmer train
Of wiser thoughts and feelings blot
Our passions from our brain;

But each day brings its petty dust
Our soon-chok'd souls to fill,   10
And we forget because we must,
And not because we will.

I struggle towards the light; and ye,
Once-long'd-for storms of love!
If with the light ye cannot be,
I bear that ye remove.

I struggle towards the light; but oh,
While yet the night is chill,
Upon Time's barren, stormy flow,
Stay with me, Marguerite, still!   20

To Marguerite, in returning a volume of the Letters of Ortis

Yes: in the sea of life enisl'd,
With echoing straits between us thrown,
Dotting the shoreless watery wild,
We mortal millions live *alone*.
  The islands feel the enclasping flow,
  And then their endless bounds they know.

But when the moon their hollows lights
And they are swept by balms of spring,
And in their glens, on starry nights,
The nightingales divinely sing;   10
And lovely notes, from shore to shore,
Across the sounds and channels pour;

Oh then a longing like despair
Is to their farthest caverns sent;
For surely once, they feel, we were
Parts of a single continent.
Now round us spreads the watery plain—
Oh might our marges meet again!

Who order'd, that their longing's fire
Should be, as soon as kindled, cool'd?   20
Who renders vain their deep desire?—
  A God, a God their severance rul'd;
And bade betwixt their shores to be
The unplumb'd, salt, estranging sea.

Memorial Verses

APRIL 1850

GOETHE in Weimar sleeps, and Greece,
Long since, saw Byron's struggle cease.
But one such death remain'd to come,
The last poetic voice is dumb
We stand to-day by Wordsworth's tomb.

When Byron's eyes were shut in death,
We bow'd our head and held our breath.
He taught us little: but our soul
Had *felt* him like the thunder's roll.
With shivering heart the strife we saw   10
Of Passion with Eternal Law;
And yet with reverential awe
We watch'd the fount of fiery life
Which serv'd for that Titanic strife.

When Goethe's death was told, we said—
Sunk, then, is Europe's sagest head.
Physician of the Iron Age,
Goethe has done his pilgrimage.
He took the suffering human race,
He read each wound, each weakness clear—   20
And struck his finger on the place
And said—Thou ailest here, and here.—
He look'd on Europe's dying hour
Of fitful dream and feverish power;
His eye plung'd down the weltering strife,
The turmoil of expiring life;
He said—The end is everywhere:
Art still has truth, take refuge there.
And he was happy, if to know
Causes of things, and far below   30
His feet to see the lurid flow
Of terror, and insane distress,
And headlong fate, be happiness.

And Wordsworth!—Ah, pale Ghosts, rejoice!
For never has such soothing voice
Been to your shadowy world convey'd,
Since erst, at morn, some wandering shade
Heard the clear song of Orpheus come
Through Hades, and the mournful gloom.
Wordsworth has gone from us—and ye,   40
Ah, may ye feel his voice as we.
He too upon a wintry clime
Had fallen—on this iron time
Of doubts, disputes, distractions, fears.
He found us when the age had bound
Our souls in its benumbing round;
He spoke, and loos'd our heart in tears.
He laid us as we lay at birth

On the cool flowery lap of earth;
Smiles broke from us and we had ease. 50
The hills were round us, and the breeze
Went o'er the sun-lit fields again:
Our foreheads felt the wind and rain.
Our youth return'd: for there was shed
On spirits that had long been dead,
Spirits dried up and closely-furl'd,
The freshness of the early world.

Ah, since dark days still bring to light
Man's prudence and man's fiery might,
Time may restore us in his course 60
Goethe's sage mind and Byron's force:
But where will Europe's latter hour
Again find Wordsworth's healing power?
Others will teach us how to dare,
And against fear our breast to steel:
Others will strengthen us to bear—
But who, ah who, will make us feel?
The cloud of mortal destiny,
Others will front it fearlessly—
But who, like him, will put it by? 70

Keep fresh the grass upon his grave,
O Rotha! with thy living wave.
Sing him thy best! for few or none
Hears thy voice right, now he is gone.

A Summer Night

IN the deserted moon-blanch'd street
How lonely rings the echo of my feet!
Those windows, which I gaze at, frown,

35

Silent and white, unopening down,
Repellent as the world:—but see!
A break between the housetops shows
The moon, and, lost behind her, fading dim
Into the dewy dark obscurity
Down at the far horizon's rim,
    Doth a whole tract of heaven disclose.   10

    And to my mind the thought
Is on a sudden brought
Of a past night, and a far different scene.
Headlands stood out into the moon-lit deep
As clearly as at noon;
The spring-tide's brimming flow
Heav'd dazzlingly between;
Houses with long white sweep
Girdled the glistening bay:
Behind, through the soft air,   20
The blue haze-cradled mountains spread away.
    That night was far more fair;
But the same restless pacings to and fro,
And the same vainly-throbbing heart was there,
And the same bright calm moon.

    And the calm moonlight seems to say—
Hast thou then still the old unquiet breast
Which neither deadens into rest
Nor ever feels the fiery glow
That whirls the spirit from itself away,   30
But fluctuates to and fro
Never by passion quite possess'd
And never quite benumb'd by the world's sway?—
And I, I know not if to pray
Still to be what I am, or yield, and be
Like all the other men I see.

For most men in a brazen prison live,
Where in the sun's hot eye,
With heads bent o'er their toil, they languidly
Their lives to some unmeaning taskwork give,   40
Dreaming of naught beyond their prison wall.
And as, year after year,
Fresh products of their barren labour fall
From their tired hands, and rest
Never yet comes more near,
Gloom settles slowly down over their breast.
And while they try to stem
The waves of mournful thought by which they are
      prest,
Death in their prison reaches them
Unfreed, having seen nothing, still unblest.   50

      And the rest, a few,
Escape their prison, and depart
On the wide Ocean of Life anew.
There the freed prisoner, where'er his heart
Listeth, will sail;
Nor doth he know how there prevail,
Despotic on that sea,
Trade-winds which cross it from eternity.
   Awhile he holds some false way, undebarr'd
By thwarting signs, and braves   60
The freshening wind and blackening waves.
And then the tempest strikes him, and between
The lightning bursts is seen
Only a driving wreck,
And the pale Master on his spar-strewn deck
With anguish'd face and flying hair
Grasping the rudder hard,
Still bent to make some port he knows not where,
Still standing for some false impossible shore.

And sterner comes the roar   70
Of sea and wind, and through the deepening gloom
Fainter and fainter wreck and helmsman loom,
And he too disappears, and comes no more.

Is there no life, but these alone?
Madman or slave, must man be one?

Plainness and clearness without shadow of stain!
Clearness divine!
Ye Heavens, whose pure dark regions have no sign
Of languor, though so calm, and though so great
Are yet untroubled and unpassionate: 80
Who though so noble share in the world's toil,
And though so task'd keep free from dust and soil:
I will not say that your mild deeps retain
A tinge, it may be, of their silent pain
Who have long'd deeply once, and long'd in vain;
But I will rather say that you remain
A world above man's head, to let him see
How boundless might his soul's horizons be,
How vast, yet of what clear transparency.
How it were good to abide there, and breathe free.   90
How fair a lot to fill
Is left to each man still.

Lines written in Kensington Gardens

IN this lone open glade I lie,
Screen'd by deep boughs on either hand;
And at its head, to stay the eye,
Those black-crown'd, red-boled pine-trees stand.

38

Birds here make song, each bird has his,
Across the girdling city's hum.
How green under the boughs it is!
How thick the tremulous sheep-cries come!

Sometimes a child will cross the glade
To take his nurse his broken toy;   10
Sometimes a thrush flit overhead
Deep in her unknown day's employ.

Here at my feet what wonders pass,
What endless, active life is here!
What blowing daisies, fragrant grass!
An air-stirr'd forest, fresh and clear.

Scarce fresher is the mountain sod
Where the tired angler lies, stretch'd out,
And, eased of basket and of rod,
Counts his day's spoil, the spotted trout.   20

In the huge world which roars hard by
Be others happy, if they can!
But in my helpless cradle I·
Was breathed on by the rural Pan.

I, on men's impious uproar hurl'd,
Think often, as I hear them rave,
That peace has left the upper world,
And now keeps only in the grave.

Yet here is peace for ever new!
When I, who watch them, am away,   30
Still all things in this glade go through
The changes of their quiet day.

Then to their happy rest they pass;
The flowers close, the birds are fed,
The night comes down upon the grass,
The child sleeps warmly in his bed.

Calm soul of all things! make it mine
To feel, amid the city's jar,
That there abides a peace of thine,
Man did not make, and cannot mar! 40

The will to neither strive nor cry,
The power to feel with others give!
Calm, calm me more! nor let me die
Before I have begun to live.

Morality

WE cannot kindle when we will
The fire which in the heart resides,
The spirit bloweth and is still,
In mystery our soul abides:
   But tasks in hours of insight will'd
Can be through hours of gloom fulfill'd.

With aching hands and bleeding feet
We dig and heap, lay stone on stone;
We bear the burden and the heat
Of the long day, and wish 'twere done. 10
   Not till the hours of light return
All we have built do we discern.

Then, when the clouds are off the soul,
When thou dost bask in Nature's eye,
Ask, how *she* view'd thy self-control,
Thy struggling task'd morality.
    Nature, whose free, light, cheerful air,
Oft made thee, in thy gloom, despair.

And she, whose censure thou dost dread,
Whose eye thou wast afraid to seek,   20
See, on her face a glow is spread,
A strong emotion on her cheek.
    'Ah child,' she cries, 'that strife divine—
Whence was it, for it is not mine?

'There is no effort on *my* brow—
I do not strive, I do not weep.
I rush with the swift spheres, and glow
In joy, and, when I will, I sleep.—
    Yet that severe, that earnest air,
I saw, I felt it once—but where?   30

'I knew not yet the gauge of Time,
Nor wore the manacles of Space.
I felt it in some other clime—
I saw it in some other place.
    —'Twas when the heavenly house I trod.
And lay upon the breast of God.'

POEMS FROM THE 1853 VOLUME

FROM

Sohrab and Rustum

Sohrab was son of Rustum, ruler of Persia, by an early love affair. However Rustum, having lost trace of Sohrab's mother, had heard rumours that the child was a girl. As a young man Sohrab joined the Tartars, who were at war with Persia, and issued a challenge to his father's army. Rustum decided to represent the Persians, but in disguise, so that unknown to each other father and son meet in single combat.

After the fight was started, Sohrab proposes a truce, but Rustum refuses:

> HE ceas'd: but while he spake, Rustum had risen,
> And stood erect, trembling with rage: his club
>   He left to lie, but had regain'd his spear,
> Whose fiery point now in his mail'd right-hand
> Blaz'd bright and baleful, like that autumn Star,
> The baleful sign of fevers: dust had soil'd
> His stately crest, and dimm'd his glittering arms.
> His breast heav'd; his lips foam'd; and twice his voice
> Was chok'd with rage: at last these words broke way:—
>   'Girl! nimble with thy feet, not with thy hands!   10
> Curl'd minion, dancer, coiner of sweet words!
> Fight; let me hear thy hateful voice no more!
> Thou art not in Afrasiab's gardens now
> With Tartar girls, with whom thou art wont to dance;
> But on the Oxus sands, and in the dance

Of battle, and with me, who make no play
Of war: I fight it out, and hand to hand.
Speak not to me of truce, and pledge, and wine!
Remember all thy valour: try thy feints
And cunning: all the pity I had is gone: 20
Because thou hast sham'd me before both the hosts
With thy light skipping tricks, and thy girl's wiles.'
    He spoke; and Sohrab kindled at his taunts,
And he too drew his sword: at once they rush'd
Together, as two eagles on one prey
Come rushing down together from the clouds,
One from the east, one from the west: their shields
Dash'd with a clang together, and a din
Rose, such as that the sinewy woodcutters
Make often in the forest's heart at morn,   30
Of hewing axes, crashing trees: such blows
Rustum and Sohrab on each other hail'd.
And you would say that sun and stars took part
In that unnatural conflict; for a cloud
Grew suddenly in Heaven, and dark'd the sun
Over the fighters' heads; and a wind rose
Under their feet, and moaning swept the plain,
And in a sandy whirlwind wrapp'd the pair.
In gloom they twain were wrapp'd, and they alone;
For both the on-looking hosts on either hand   40
Stood in broad daylight, and the sky was pure,
And the sun sparkled on the Oxus stream.
But in the gloom they fought, with bloodshot eyes
And labouring breath; first Rustum struck the shield
Which Sohrab held stiff out: the steel-spik'd spear
Rent the tough plates, but fail'd to reach the skin,
And Rustum pluck'd it back with angry groan.
Then Sohrab with his sword smote Rustum's helm,
Nor clove its steel quite through; but all the crest
He shore away, and that proud horsehair plume   50

43

Never till now defil'd, sunk to the dust;
And Rustum bow'd his head; but then the gloom
Grew blacker: thunder rumbled in the air,
And lightnings rent the cloud; and Ruksh, the horse,
Who stood at hand, utter'd a dreadful cry:
No horse's cry was that, most like the roar
Of some pain'd desert lion, who all day
Has trail'd the hunter's javelin in his side,
And comes at night to die upon the sand:—
The two hosts heard that cry, and quak'd for fear,   60
And Oxus curdled as it cross'd his stream.
But Sohrab heard, and quail'd not, but rush'd on,
And struck again; and again Rustum bow'd
His head; but this time all the blade, like glass,
Sprang in a thousand shivers on the helm,
And in his hand the hilt remain'd alone.
Then Rustum rais'd his head: his dreadful eyes
Glar'd, and he shook on high his menacing spear,
And shouted, *Rustum!* Sohrab heard that shout.
And shrank amaz'd: back he recoil'd one step,   70
And scann'd with blinking eyes the advancing Form:
And then he stood bewilder'd; and he dropp'd
His covering shield, and the spear pierc'd his side.
He reel'd, and staggering back, sunk to the ground.
And then the gloom dispers'd, and the wind fell,
And the bright sun broke forth, and melted all
The cloud; and the two armies saw the pair;
Saw Rustum standing, safe upon his feet,
And Sohrab, wounded, on the bloody sand.

    Then, with a bitter smile, Rustum began:—   80
'Sohrab, thou thoughtest in thy mind to kill
A Persian lord this day, and strip his corpse,
And bear thy trophies to Afrasiab's tent.
Or else that the great Rustum would come down
Himself to fight, and that thy wiles would move

His heart to take a gift, and let thee go.
And then that all the Tartar host would praise
Thy courage or thy craft, and spread thy fame,
To glad thy father in his weak old age.
Fool! thou art slain, and by an unknown man!   90
Dearer to the red jackals shalt thou be,
Than to thy friends, and to thy father old.'
    And, with a fearless mien, Sohrab replied:—
'Unknown thou art; yet thy fierce vaunt is vain.
Thou dost not slay me, proud and boastful man!
No! Rustum slays me, and this filial heart.
For were I match'd with ten such men as thou,
And I were he who till to-day I was,
They should be lying here, I standing there.
But that belovèd name unnerv'd my arm—   100
That name, and something, I confess, in thee,
Which troubles all my heart, and made my shield
Fall; and thy spear transfix'd an unarm'd foe.
And now thou boastest, and insult'st my fate.
But hear thou this, fierce Man, tremble to hear!
The mighty Rustum shall avenge my death!
My father, whom I seek through all the world,
He shall avenge my death, and punish thee!'
    As when some hunter in the spring hath found
A breeding eagle sitting on her nest,
Upon the craggy isle of a hill lake,   110
And pierc'd her with an arrow as she rose,
And follow'd her to find her where she fell
Far off;—anon her mate comes winging back
From hunting, and a great way off descries
His huddling young left sole; at that, he checks
His pinion, and with short uneasy sweeps
Circles above his eyry, with loud screams
Chiding his mate back to her nest; but she
Lies dying, with the arrow in her side,   120

45

In some far stony gorge out of his ken,
A heap of fluttering feathers: never more
Shall the lake glass her, flying over it;
Never the black and dripping precipices
Echo her stormy scream as she sails by:—
As that poor bird flies home, nor knows his loss—
So Rustum knew not his own loss, but stood
Over his dying son, and knew him not.

But with a cold, incredulous voice, he said:—
'What prate is this of fathers and revenge?   130
The mighty Rustum never had a son.'

And, with a failing voice, Sohrab replied:—
'Ah yes, he had! and that lost son am I.
Surely the news will one day reach his ear,
Reach Rustum, where he sits, and tarries long,
Somewhere, I know not where, but far from here;
And pierce him like a stab, and make him leap
To arms, and cry for vengeance upon thee.
Fierce Man, bethink thee, for an only son!
What will that grief, what will that vengeance be!   140
Oh, could I live, till I that grief had seen!
Yet him I pity not so much, but her,
My mother, who in Ader-baijan dwells
With that old King, her father, who grows grey
With age, and rules over the valiant Koords.
Her most I pity, who no more will see
Sohrab returning from the Tartar camp,
With spoils and honour, when the war is done.
But a dark rumour will be bruited up,
From tribe to tribe, until it reach her ear;   150
And then will that defenceless woman learn
That Sohrab will rejoice her sight no more;
But that in battle with a nameless foe,
By the far-distant Oxus, he is slain.'

He spoke; and as he ceas'd he wept aloud,

46

Thinking of her he left, and his own death. . . .
And Rustum gaz'd on him with grief, and said:—
  'O Sohrab, thou indeed art such a son
Whom Rustum, wert thou his, might well have lov'd!
Yet here thou errest, Sohrab, or else men   160
Have told thee false;—thou art not Rustum's son.
For Rustum had no son: one child he had—
But one—a girl: who with her mother now
Plies some light female task, nor dreams of us—
Of us she dreams not, nor of wounds, nor war.'
  But Sohrab answer'd him in wrath; for now
The anguish of the deep-fix'd spear grew fierce,
And he desired to draw forth the steel,
And let the blood flow free, and so to die;
But first he would convince his stubborn foe—   170
And, rising sternly on one arm, he said:—
  'Man, who art thou who dost deny my words?
Truth sits upon the lips of dying men,
And Falsehood, while I liv'd, was far from mine.
I tell thee, prick'd upon this arm I bear
That seal which Rustum to my mother gave,
That she might prick it on the babe she bore.'
  He spoke: and all the blood left Rustum's cheeks;
And his knees totter'd, and he smote his hand
Against his breast, his heavy mailed hand,   180
That the hard iron corslet clank'd aloud:
And to his heart he press'd the other hand,
And in a hollow voice he spake, and said:—
  'Sohrab, that were a proof which could not lie.
If thou shew this, then art thou Rustum's son.'
  Then, with weak hasty fingers, Sohrab loos'd
His belt, and near the shoulder bar'd his arm,
And shew'd a sign in faint vermilion points
Prick'd: as a cunning workman, in Pekin,
Pricks with vermilion some clear porcelain vase,   190

An emperor's gift—at early morn he paints,
And all day long, and, when night comes, the lamp
Lights up his studious forehead and thin hands:—
So delicately prick'd the sign appear'd
Oh Sohrab's arm, the sign of Rustum's seal.
It was that Griffin, which of old rear'd Zal,
Rustum's great father, whom they left to die,
A helpless babe, among the mountain rocks.
Him that kind Creature found, and rear'd, and lov'd—
Then Rustum took it for his glorious sign.   200
And Sohrab bar'd that figure on his arm,
And himself scann'd it long with mournful eyes,
And then he touch'd it with his hand and said:—

   'How say'st thou? Is that sign the proper sign
Of Rustum's son, or of some other man's?'

   He spoke: but Rustum gaz'd, and gaz'd, and stood
Speechless; and then he utter'd one sharp cry—
O Boy—thy Father!—and his voice chok'd there.

.   .   .   .

   He spoke; and Sohrab smil'd on him, and took
The spear, and drew it from his side, and eas'd   210
His wound's imperious anguish: but the blood
Came welling from the open gash, and life
Flow'd with the stream: all down his cold white side
The crimson torrent ran, dim now, and soil'd,
Like the soil'd tissue of white violets
Left, freshly gather'd, on their native bank,
By romping children, whom their nurses call
From the hot fields at noon: his head droop'd low,
His limbs grew slack; motionless, white, he lay—
White, with eyes closed; only when heavy gasps,   220
Deep, heavy gasps, quivering through all his frame,
Convuls'd him back to life, he open'd them,
And fix'd them feebly on his father's face:
Till now all strength was ebb'd, and from his limbs

Unwillingly the spirit fled away,
Regretting the warm mansion which it left,
And youth and bloom, and this delightful world.
  So, on the bloody sand, Sohrab lay dead.
And the great Rustum drew his horseman's cloak
Down o'er his face, and sate by his dead son.   230
As those black granite pillars, once high-rear'd
By Jemshid in Persepolis, to bear
His house, now, mid their broken flights of steps,
Lie prone, enormous, down the mountain side—
So in the sand lay Rustum by his son.
  And night came down over the solemn waste,
And the two gazing hosts, and that sole pair,
And darken'd all; and a cold fog, with night,
Crept from the Oxus. Soon a hum arose,
As of a great assembly loos'd, and fires   240
Began to twinkle through the fog: for now
Both armies mov'd to camp, and took their meal:
The Persians took it on the open sands
Southward; the Tartars by the river marge;
And Rustum and his son were left alone.
  But the majestic River floated on,
Out of the mist and hum of that low land,
Into the frosty starlight, and there mov'd,
Rejoicing, through the hush'd Chorasmian waste,
Under the solitary moon: he flow'd   250
Right for the Polar Star, past Orgunjè,
Brimming, and bright, and large: then sands begin
To hem his watery march, and dam his streams,
And split his currents; that for many a league
The shorn and parcell'd Oxus strains along
Through beds of sand and matted rushy isles—
Oxus, forgetting the bright speed he had
In his high mountain cradle in Pamere,
A foil'd circuitous wanderer:—till at last

The long'd-for dash of waves is heard, and wide   260
His luminous home of waters opens, bright
And tranquil, from whose floor the new-bath'd stars
Emerge, and shine upon the Aral Sea.

Philomela

HARK! ah, the Nightingale!
The tawny-throated!
Hark! from that moonlit cedar what a burst!
What triumph! hark—what pain!

O Wanderer from a Grecian shore,
Still, after many years, in distant lands,
Still nourishing in thy bewilder'd brain
That wild, unquench'd, deep-sunken, old-world pain—
    Say, will it never heal?
And can this fragrant lawn   10
With its cool trees, and night,
And the sweet, tranquil Thames,
And moonshine, and the dew,
To thy rack'd heart and brain
    Afford no balm?

    Dost thou to-night behold
Here, through the moonlight on this English grass,
The unfriendly palace in the Thracian wild?
    Dost thou again peruse
With hot cheeks and sear'd eyes   20
The too clear web, and thy dumb sister's shame?
    Dost thou once more assay
Thy flight, and feel come over thee,

50

Poor fugitive, the feathery change
Once more, and once more seem to make resound
With love and hate, triumph and agony,
Lone Daulis, and the high Cephissian vale?
   Listen, Eugenia—
How thick the bursts come crowding through the leaves!
   Again—thou hearest!   30
Eternal passion!
Eternal pain!

Requiescat

S TREW on her roses, roses,
   And never a spray of yew.
In quiet she reposes:
   Ah! would that I did too.

Her mirth the world required:
   She bath'd it in smiles of glee.
But her heart was tired, tired,
   And now they let her be.

Her life was turning, turning,
   In mazes of heat and sound.   10
But for peace her soul was yearning,
   And now peace laps her round.

Her cabin'd, ample Spirit,
   It flutter'd and fail'd for breath.
To-night it doth inherit
   The vasty Hall of Death.

The Scholar Gipsy

Go for they call you, Shepherd, from the hill;
  Go, Shepherd, and untie the wattled cotes:
    No longer leave thy wistful flock unfed,
  Nor let thy bawling fellows rack their throats,
    Nor the cropp'd herbage shoot another head.
      But when the fields are still,
  And the tired men and dogs all gone to rest,
    And only the white sheep are sometimes seen
    Cross and recross the stripes of moon-blanch'd green;
    Come, Shepherd, and again begin the quest.   10

Here, where the reaper was at work of late,
  In this high field's dark corner, where he leaves
    His coat, his basket, and his earthen cruise,
  And in the sun all morning binds the sheaves,
    Then here, at noon, comes back his stores to use;
      Here will I sit and wait,
  While to my ear from uplands far away
    The bleating of the folded flocks is borne,
    With distant cries of reapers in the corn—
    All the live murmur of a summer's day.   20

Screen'd is this nook o'er the high, half-reap'd field,
  And here till sun-down, Shepherd, will I be.
    Through the thick corn the scarlet poppies peep,
  And round green roots and yellowing stalks I see
    Pale pink convolvulus in tendrils creep:
      And air-swept lindens yield

Their scent, and rustle down their perfum'd showers
    Of bloom on the bent grass where I am laid,
      And bower me from the August sun with shade;
        And the eye travels down to Oxford's towers: 30

And near me on the grass lies Glanvil's book—
    Come, let me read the oft-read tale again,
      The story of the Oxford scholar poor
    Of pregnant parts and quick inventive brain,
      Who, tir'd of knocking at Preferment's door,
        One summer morn forsook
His friends, and went to learn the Gipsy Lore,
    And roam'd the world with that wild brotherhood,
    And came, as most men deem'd, to little good,
      But came to Oxford and his friends no more.   40

But once, years after, in the country lanes,
    Two scholars whom at college erst he knew
      Met him, and of his way of life inquir'd.
    Whereat he answer'd, that the Gipsy crew,
      His mates, had arts to rule as they desir'd
        The workings of men's brains;
And they can bind them to what thoughts they will:
    'And I,' he said, 'the secret of their art,
    When fully learn'd, will to the world impart:
      But it needs heaven-sent moments for this skill.'   50

This said, he left them, and return'd no more,
    But rumours hung about the country side
      That the lost Scholar long was seen to stray,
    Seen by rare glimpses, pensive and tongue-tied,
      In hat of antique shape, and cloak of grey,
        The same the Gipsies wore.
Shepherds had met him on the Hurst in spring;

At some lone alehouse in the Berkshire moors,
  On the warm ingle bench, the smock-frock'd boors
    Had found him seated at their entering,   60

But, mid their drink and clatter, he would fly:
  And I myself seem half to know thy looks,
    And put the shepherds, Wanderer, on thy trace;
  And boys who in lone wheatfields scare the rooks
    I ask if thou hast pass'd their quiet place;
      Or in my boat I lie
  Moor'd to the cool bank in the summer heats,
    Mid wide grass meadows which the sunshine fills,
    And watch the warm green-muffled Cumner hills,
      And wonder if thou haunt'st their shy retreats.   70

For most, I know, thou lov'st retired ground.
  Thee, at the ferry, Oxford riders blithe,
    Returning home on summer nights, have met
  Crossing the stripling Thames at Bab-lock-hithe,
    Trailing in the cool stream thy fingers wet,
      As the punt's rope chops round:
  And leaning backward in a pensive dream,
    And fostering in thy lap a heap of flowers
  Pluck'd in shy fields and distant Wychwood bowers,
      And thine eyes resting on the moonlit stream: 80

And then they land, and thou art seen no more.
  Maidens who from the distant hamlets come
    To dance around the Fyfield elm in May,
  Oft through the darkening fields have seen thee roam,
    Or cross a stile into the public way.
      Oft thou hast given them store
  Of flowers—the frail-leaf'd, white anemone—
    Dark bluebells drench'd with dews of summer eves—
    And purple orchises with spotted leaves—
      But none hath words she can report of thee.   90

And, above Godstow Bridge, when hay-time's here
    In June, and many a scythe in sunshine flames,
        Men who through those wide fields of breezy grass
    Where black-wing'd swallows haunt the glittering Thames,
        To bathe in the abandon'd lasher pass,
            Have often pass'd thee near
    Sitting upon the river bank o'ergrown:
        Mark'd thine outlandish garb, thy figure spare,
        Thy dark vague eyes, and soft abstracted air;
            But, when they came from bathing, thou wast gone.   100

At some lone homestead in the Cumner hills,
    Where at her open door the housewife darns,
        Thou hast been seen, or hanging on a gate
    To watch the threshers in the mossy barns.
        Children, who early range these slopes and late
            For cresses from the rills,
    Have known thee eying, all an April day,
        The springing pastures and the feeding kine;
        And mark'd thee, when the stars come out and shine,
            Through the long dewy grass move slow away.   110

In Autumn, on the skirts of Bagley wood,
    Where most the Gipsies by the turf-edg'd way
        Pitch their smok'd tents, and every bush you see
    With scarlet patches tagg'd and shreds of grey,
        Above the forest ground call'd Thessaly—
            The blackbird picking food
    Sees thee, nor stops his meal, nor fears at all;
        So often has he known thee past him stray
        Rapt, twirling in thy hand a wither'd spray,
            And waiting for the spark from Heaven to fall.   120

And once, in winter, on the causeway chill
    Where home through flooded fields foot-travellers go,

Have I not pass'd thee on the wooden bridge
Wrapt in thy cloak and battling with the snow,
   Thy face tow'rd Hinksey and its wintry ridge?
     And thou hast climb'd the hill
And gain'd the white brow of the Cumner range,
   Turn'd once to watch, while thick the snowflakes fall,
   The line of festal light in Christ-Church hall—
     Then sought thy straw in some sequester'd grange.   130

But what—I dream! Two hundred years are flown
   Since first thy story ran through Oxford halls,
     And the grave Glanvil did the tale inscribe
That thou wert wander'd from the studious walls
   To learn strange arts, and join a Gipsy tribe:
     And thou from earth art gone
Long since, and in some quiet churchyard laid;
   Some country nook, where o'er thy unknown grave
   Tall grasses and white flowering nettles wave—
     Under a dark red-fruited yew-tree's shade.   140

—No, no, thou hast not felt the lapse of hours.
   For what wears out the life of mortal men?
     'Tis that from change to change their being rolls:
   'Tis that repeated shocks, again, again,
     Exhaust the energy of strongest souls,
       And numb the elastic powers.
Till having us'd our nerves with bliss and teen,
   And tir'd upon a thousand schemes our wit,
   To the just-pausing Genius we remit
     Our worn-out life, and are—what we have been.   150

Thou hast not liv'd, why should'st thou perish, so?
   Thou hadst *one* aim, *one* business, *one* desire:
     Else wert thou long since number'd with the dead—
     Else hadst thou spent, like other men, thy fire.

The generations of thy peers are fled,
    And we ourselves shall go;
But thou possessest an immortal lot,
    And we imagine thee exempt from age
    And living as thou liv'st on Glanvil's page,
        Because thou hadst—what we, alas, have not!   160

For early didst thou leave the world, with powers
    Fresh, undiverted to the world without,
        Firm to their mark, not spent on other things;
    Free from the sick fatigue, the languid doubt,
        Which much to have tried, in much been baffled, brings.
            O Life unlike to ours!
    Who fluctuate idly without term or scope,
        Of whom each strives, nor knows for what he strives,
        And each half lives a hundred different lives;
            Who wait like thee, but not, like thee, in hope.   170

Thou waitest for the spark from Heaven: and we,
    Light half-believers of our casual creeds,
        Who never deeply felt, nor clearly will'd,
    Whose insight never has borne fruit in deeds,
        Whose vague resolves never have been fulfill'd;
            For whom each year we see
    Breeds new beginnings, disappointments new;
        Who hesitate and falter life away,
        And lose to-morrow the ground won to-day—
            Ah, do not we, Wanderer, await it too?   180

Yes, we await it, but it still delays,
    And then we suffer; and amongst us One,
        Who most has suffer'd, takes dejectedly
    His seat upon the intellectual throne;
        And all his store of sad experience he
            Lays bare of wretched days;

Tells us his misery's birth and growth and signs,
    And how the dying spark of hope was fed,
    And how the breast was sooth'd, and how the head,
        And all his hourly varied anodynes.   190

This for our wisest: and we others pine,
    And wish the long unhappy dream would end,
    And waive all claim to bliss, and try to bear,
    With close-lipp'd Patience for our only friend,
        Sad Patience, too near neighbour to Despair:
            But none has hope like thine.
    Thou through the fields and through the woods dost stray,
        Roaming the country side, a truant boy,
        Nursing thy project in unclouded joy,
            And every doubt long blown by time away.   200

O born in days when wits were fresh and clear,
    And life ran gaily as the sparkling Thames;
        Before this strange disease of modern life,
    With its sick hurry, its divided aims,
        Its heads o'ertax'd, its palsied hearts, was rife—
            Fly hence, our contact fear!
    Still fly, plunge deeper in the bowering wood!
        Averse, as Dido did with gesture stern
        From her false friend's approach in Hades turn,
            Wave us away, and keep thy solitude.   210

Still nursing the unconquerable hope,
    Still clutching the inviolable shade,
        With a free onward impulse brushing through,
    By night, the silver'd branches of the glade—
        Far on the forest skirts, where none pursue,
            On some mild pastoral slope
    Emerge, and resting on the moonlit pales,

Freshen thy flowers, as in former years,
With dew, or listen with enchanted ears,
From the dark dingles, to the nightingales.   220

But fly our paths, our feverish contact fly!
For strong the infection of our mental strife,
Which, though it gives no bliss, yet spoils for rest;
And we should win thee from thy own fair life,
Like us distracted, and like us unblest.
Soon, soon thy cheer would die,
Thy hopes grow timorous, and unfix'd thy powers,
And thy clear aims be cross and shifting made:
And then thy glad perennial youth would fade,
Fade, and grow old at last, and die like ours.   230

Then fly our greetings, fly our speech and smiles!
—As some grave Tyrian trader, from the sea,
Descried at sunrise an emerging prow
Lifting the cool-hair'd creepers stealthily,
The fringes of a southward-facing brow
Among the Aegean isles;
And saw the merry Grecian coaster come,
Freighted with amber grapes, and Chian wine,
Green bursting figs, and tunnies steep'd in brine;
And knew the intruders on his ancient home.   240

The young light-hearted Masters of the waves;
And snatch'd his rudder, and shook out more sail,
And day and night held on indignantly
O'er the blue Midland waters with the gale,
Betwixt the Syrtes and soft Sicily,
To where the Atlantic raves
Outside the Western Straits, and unbent sails
There, where down cloudy cliffs, through sheets of foam,
Shy traffickers, the dark Iberians come;
And on the beach undid his corded bales.   250

The 'Death' of Aepytus

(FROM *Merope*)

Aepytus returns in disguise to revenge himself on Polyphontes, the murderer of his father and usurper of his throne. He gains admission to the court by pretending to be a messenger bringing news of Aepytus' death. Here he describes how he met his 'death' on a hunting expedition:

There is a chasm rifted in the base
Of that unfooted precipice, whose rock
Walls on one side the deep Stymphalian Lake:
There the lake-waters, which in ages gone
Wash'd, as the marks upon the hills still show,
All the Stymphalian plain, are now suck'd down.
A headland, with one agèd plane-tree crown'd,
Parts from the cave-pierc'd cliff the shelving bay
Where first the chase plung'd in: the bay is smooth,
But round the headland's point a current sets,   10
Strong, black, tempestuous, to the cavern-mouth.
Stoutly, under the headland's lee, they swam:
But when they came abreast the point, the race
Caught them, as wind takes feathers, whirl'd them round
Struggling in vain to cross it, swept them on,
Stag, dogs, and hunter, to the yawning gulph.
All this, O King, not piecemeal, as to thee
Now told, but in one flashing instant pass'd:
While from the turf whereon I lay I sprang,
And took three strides, quarry and dogs were gone;   20
A moment more—I saw the prince turn round
Once in the black and arrowy race, and cast

One arm aloft for help; then sweep beneath
The low-brow'd cavern-arch, and disappear.
And what I could, I did—to call by cries
Some straggling hunters to my aid, to rouse
Fishers who live on the lake-side, to launch
Boats, and approach, near as we dar'd, the chasm.
But of the prince nothing remain'd, save this,
His boar-spear's broken shaft, back on the lake   30
Cast by the rumbling subterranean stream;
And this, at landing spied by us and sav'd,
His broad-brimm'd hunter's hat, which, in the bay,
Where first the stag took water, floated still.
And I across the mountains brought with haste
. . . this news. . . .

POEMS FROM THE 1867 VOLUME

Thyrsis

A MONODY, *to commemorate the author's friend*, ARTHUR
HUGH CLOUGH, *who died at Florence*, 1861

HOW changed is here each spot man makes or fills!
    In the two Hinkseys nothing keeps the same;
        The village-street its haunted mansion lacks,
    And from the sign is gone Sibylla's name,
        And from the roofs the twisted chimney-stacks;
            Are ye too changed, ye hills?
    See, 'tis no foot of unfamiliar men
        To-night from Oxford up your pathway strays.
        Here came I often, in old days;
    Thyrsis and I; we still had Thyrsis then.   10

61

Runs it not here, the track by Childsworth Farm,
　　Past the high wood, to where the elm-tree crowns
　　　The hill behind whose ridge the sunset flames?
The signal-elm, that looks on Ilsley Downs,
　　The Vale, the three lone weirs, the youthful Thames?—
　　　This winter-eve is warm,
Humid the air; leafless, yet soft as spring,
　　The tender purple spray on copse and briers;
　　And that sweet City with her dreaming spires,
She needs not June for beauty's heightening.　　　20

Lovely all times she lies, lovely to-night!
　　Only, methinks, some loss of habit's power
　　　Befalls me wandering through this upland dim;
Once pass'd I blindfold here, at any hour,
　　Now seldom come I, since I came with him.
　　　That single elm-tree bright
Against the west—I miss it! is it gone?
　　We prized it dearly; while it stood, we said,
　　Our friend, the Scholar-Gipsy, was not dead;
While the tree lived, he in these fields lived on.　　　30

Too rare, too rare, grow now my visits here!
　　But once I knew each field, each flower, each stick;
　　　And with the country-folk acquaintance made
By barn in threshing-time, by new-built rick.
　　Here, too, our shepherd-pipes we first assay'd.
　　　Ah me! this many a year
My pipe is lost, my shepherd's-holiday!
　　Needs must I lose them, needs with heavy heart
　　Into the world and wave of men depart;
But Thyrsis of his own will went away.　　　40

It irk'd him to be here, he could not rest.
　　He loved each simple joy the country yields,

He loved his mates; but yet he could not keep,
For that a shadow lour'd on the fields,
   Here with the shepherds and the silly sheep.
     Some life of men unblest
He knew, which made him droop, and fill'd his head.
   He went; his piping took a troubled sound
   Of storms that rage outside our happy ground;
He could not wait their passing, he is dead!   50

So, some tempestuous morn in early June,
   When the year's primal burst of bloom is o'er,
    Before the roses and the longest day—
   When garden-walks, and all the grassy floor,
    With blossoms, red and white, of fallen May,
     And chestnut-flowers are strewn—
So have I heard the cuckoo's parting cry,
   From the wet field, through the vext garden-trees,
   Come with the volleying rain and tossing breeze:
The bloom is gone, and with the bloom go I.   60

Too quick despairer, wherefore wilt thou go?
   Soon will the high Midsummer pomps come on,
    Soon will the musk carnations break and swell,
Soon shall we have gold-dusted snapdragon,
    Sweet-William with his homely cottage-smell,
     And stocks in fragrant blow;
Roses that down the alleys shine afar,
   And open, jasmine-muffled lattices,
   And groups under the dreaming garden-trees,
And the full moon, and the white evening-star.   70

He hearkens not! light comer, he is flown!
   What matters it? next year he will return,
    And we shall have him in the sweet spring-days,
   With whitening hedges, and uncrumpling fern,

And blue-bells trembling by the forest-ways,
    And scent of hay new-mown.
But Thyrsis never more we swains shall see!
    See him come back, and cut a smoother reed,
    And blow a strain the world at last shall heed—
For Time, not Corydon, hath conquer'd thee.   80

Alack, for Corydon no rival now!—
    But when Sicilian shepherds lost a mate,
        Some good survivor with his flute would go,
    Piping a ditty sad for Bion's fate,
        And cross the unpermitted ferry's flow,
            And relax Pluto's brow,
    And make leap up with joy the beauteous head
        Of Proserpine, among whose crownèd hair
        Are flowers, first open'd on Sicilian air,
    And flute his friend, like Orpheus, from the dead.   90

O easy access to the hearer's grace
    When Dorian shepherds sang to Proserpine!
        For she herself had trod Sicilian fields,
    She knew the Dorian water's gush divine,
        She knew each lily white which Enna yields,
            Each rose with blushing face;
    She loved the Dorian pipe, the Dorian strain.
        But ah, of our poor Thames she never heard!
        Her foot the Cumner cowslips never stirr'd;
    And we should tease her with our plaint in vain!   100

Well! wind-dispers'd and vain the words will be,
    Yet, Thyrsis, let me give my grief its hour
        In the old haunt, and find our tree-topp'd hill!
    Who, if not I, for questing here hath power?
        I know the wood which hides the daffodil,
            I know the Fyfield tree,

I know what white, what purple fritillaries
  The grassy harvest of the river-fields,
    Above by Ensham, down by Sandford, yields,
And what sedg'd brooks are Thames's tributaries;   110

I know these slopes; who knows them if not I?—
  But many a dingle on the loved hill-side,
    With thorns once studded, old, white-blossom'd trees,
  Where thick the cowslips grew, and, far descried,
    High tower'd the spikes of purple orchises,
      Hath since our day put by
The coronals of that forgotten time.
  Down each green bank hath gone the ploughboy's team,
  And only in the hidden brookside gleam
Primroses, orphans of the flowery prime.   120

Where is the girl, who, by the boatman's door,
  Above the locks, above the boating throng,
    Unmoor'd our skiff, when, through the Wytham flats,
  Red loosestrife and blond meadow-sweet among,
    And darting swallows, and light water-gnats,
      We track'd the shy Thames shore?
Where are the mowers, who, as the tiny swell
  Of our boat passing heav'd the river-grass,
  Stood with suspended scythe to see us pass?—
They all are gone, and thou art gone as well.   130

Yes, thou art gone! and round me too the night
  In ever-nearing circle weaves her shade.
    I see her veil draw soft across the day,
  I feel her slowly chilling breath invade
    The cheek grown thin, the brown hair sprent with grey;
      I feel her finger light
Laid pausefully upon life's headlong train;

The foot less prompt to meet the morning dew,
The heart less bounding at emotion new,
And hope, once crush'd, less quick to spring again.   140

And long the way appears, which seem'd so short
    To the less practis'd eye of sanguine youth;
        And high the mountain-tops, in cloudy air,
    The mountain-tops where is the throne of Truth,
        Tops in life's morning-sun so bright and bare!
            Unbreachable the fort
Of the long-batter'd world uplifts its wall.
    And strange and vain the earthly turmoil grows,
    And near and real the charm of thy repose,
And night as welcome as a friend would fall.   150

But hush! the upland hath a sudden loss
    Of quiet;—Look! adown the dusk hill-side,
        A troop of Oxford hunters going home,
    As in old days, jovial and talking, ride!
        From hunting with the Berkshire hounds they come—
            Quick, let me fly, and cross
Into yon farther field!—'Tis done; and see,
    Back'd by the sunset, which doth glorify
    The orange and pale violet evening-sky,
Bare on its lonely ridge, the Tree! the Tree!   160

I take the omen! Eve lets down her veil,
    The white fog creeps from bush to bush about,
        The west unflushes, the high stars grow bright,
    And in the scatter'd farms the lights come out.
        I cannot reach the Signal-Tree to-night,
            Yet, happy omen, hail!
Hear it from thy broad lucent Arno vale
    (For there thine earth-forgetting eyelids keep
    The morningless and unawakening sleep
Under the flowery oleanders pale),   170

Hear it, O Thyrsis, still our Tree is there!—
Ah, vain! These English fields, this upland dim,
These brambles pale with mist engarlanded,
That lone, sky-pointing tree, are not for him.
To a boon southern country he is fled,
And now in happier air,
Wandering with the great Mother's train divine
(And purer or more subtle soul than thee,
I trow, the mighty Mother doth not see!)
Within a folding of the Apennine,   180

Thou hearest the immortal chants of old.
Putting his sickle to the perilous grain
In the hot cornfield of the Phrygian king,
For thee the Lityerses song again
Young Daphnis with his silver voice doth sing;
Sings his Sicilian fold,
His sheep, his hapless love, his blinded eyes;
And how a call celestial round him rang
And heavenward from the fountain-brink he sprang,
And all the marvel of the golden skies.   190

There thou art gone, and me thou leavest here
Sole in these fields; yet will I not despair;
Despair I will not, while I yet descry
'Neath the mild canopy of English air
That lonely Tree against the western sky.
Still, still these slopes, 'tis clear,
Our Gipsy-Scholar haunts, outliving thee!
Fields where soft sheep from cages pull the hay,
Woods with anemonies in flower till May,
Know him a wanderer still; then why not me?   200

A fugitive and gracious light he seeks,
Shy to illumine; and I seek it too.

This does not come with houses or with gold,
With place, with honour, and a flattering crew;
'Tis not in the world's market bought and sold.
    But the smooth-slipping weeks
Drop by, and leave its seeker still untired;
    Out of the heed of mortals he is gone,
    He wends unfollow'd, he must house alone;
Yet on he fares, by his own heart inspired.   210

Thou too, O Thyrsis, on like quest wast bound,
    Thou wanderedst with me for a little hour;
        Men gave thee nothing, but this happy quest,
    If men esteem'd thee feeble, gave thee power,
        If men procured thee trouble, gave thee rest.
            And this rude Cumner ground,
        Its fir-topped Hurst, its farms, its quiet fields,
            Here cam'st thou in thy jocund youthful time,
            Here was thine height of strength, thy golden prime;
        And still the haunt beloved a virtue yields.   220

What though the music of thy rustic flute
    Kept not for long its happy, country tone,
        Lost it too soon, and learnt a stormy note
    Of men contention-tost, of men who groan,
        Which task'd thy pipe too sore, and tired thy throat—
            It fail'd, and thou wast mute;
        Yet hadst thou always visions of our light,
            And long with men of care thou couldst not stay,
            And soon thy foot resumed its wandering way,
        Left human haunt, and on alone till night.   230

Too rare, too rare, grow now my visits here!
    'Mid city-noise, not, as with thee of yore,
        Thyrsis, in reach of sheep-bells is my home!
    Then through the great town's harsh, heart-wearying roar,

68

Let in thy voice a whisper often come,
　　To chase fatigue and fear:
Why faintest thou? I wander'd till I died.
　Roam on! the light we sought is shining still.
　Dost thou ask proof? Our Tree yet crowns the hill,
Our Scholar travels yet the loved hillside.　　　　　240

Saint Brandan

SAINT BRANDAN sails the northern main;
The brotherhood of saints are glad.
He greets them once, he sails again.
So late!—such storms!—The Saint so mad!

He heard across the howling seas
Chime convent bells on wintry nights,
He saw on spray-swept Hebrides
Twinkle the monastery lights;

But north, still north, Saint Brandan steer'd;
And now no bells, no convents more!　　　　　10
The hurtling Polar lights are near'd,
The sea without a human shore.

At last—(it was the Christmas night,
Stars shone after a day of storm)—
He sees float past an iceberg white,
And on it—Christ!—a living form!

That furtive mien, that scowling eye,
Of hair that red and tufted fell——
It is—Oh, where shall Brandan fly?—
The traitor Judas, out of hell!　　　　　20

69

Palsied with terror, Brandan sate;
The moon was bright, the iceberg near.
He hears a voice sigh humbly: 'Wait!
By high permission I am here.

'One moment wait, thou holy man!
On earth my crime, my death, they knew;
My name is under all men's ban;
Ah, tell them of my respite too!

'Tell them, one blessed Christmas night—
(It was the first after I came,⁣   30
Breathing self-murder, frenzy, spite,
To rue my guilt in endless flame)—

'I felt, as I in torment lay
'Mid the souls plagued by heavenly power,
An angel touch mine arm, and say:
Go hence, and cool thyself an hour!

' "Ah, whence this mercy, Lord?" I said.
The Leper recollect, said he,
Who ask'd the passers-by for aid,
In Joppa, and thy charity.   40

'Then I remember'd how I went,
In Joppa, through the public street,
One morn, when the sirocco spent
Its storms of dust, with burning heat;

'And in the street a Leper sate,
Shivering with fever, naked, old;
Sand raked his sores from heel to pate,
The hot wind fever'd him five-fold.

70

'He gazed upon me as I pass'd,
And murmur'd: *Help me, or I die!*—   50
To the poor wretch my cloak I cast,
Saw him look eased, and hurried by.

'Oh, Brandan, think what grace divine,
What blessing must true goodness shower,
If semblance of it faint, like mine,
Hath such inestimable power!

'Well-fed, well-clothed, well-friended, I
Did that chance act of good, that one!
Then went my way to kill and lie—
Forgot my good as soon as done.   60

'That germ of kindness, in the womb
Of mercy caught, did not expire;
Outlives my guilt, outlives my doom,
And friends me in the pit of fire.

'Once every year, when carols wake,
On earth, the Christmas night's repose,
Arising from the sinners' lake,
I journey to these healing snows.

'I stanch with ice my burning breast,
With silence balm my whirling brain.   70
O Brandan! to this hour of rest
That Joppan leper's ease was pain.'

Tears started to Saint Brandan's eyes;
He bow'd his head, he breathed a prayer—
Then look'd, and lo, the frosty skies!
The iceberg, and no Judas there!

Dover Beach

The sea is calm to-night,
The tide is full, the moon lies fair
Upon the Straits;—on the French coast, the light
Gleams, and is gone; the cliffs of England stand,
Glimmering and vast, out in the tranquil bay.
Come to the window, sweet is the night air!
Only, from the long line of spray
Where the sea meets the moon-blanch'd sand,
Listen! you hear the grating roar
Of pebbles which the waves suck back, and fling,   10
At their return, up the high strand,
Begin, and cease, and then again begin,
With tremulous cadence slow, and bring
The eternal note of sadness in.

Sophocles long ago
Heard it on the Aegaean, and it brought
Into his mind the turbid ebb and flow
Of human misery; we
Find also in the sound a thought,
Hearing it by this distant northern sea.   20

The sea of faith
Was once, too, at the full, and round earth's shore
Lay like the folds of a bright girdle furl'd;
But now I only hear
Its melancholy, long, withdrawing roar,
Retreating to the breath
Of the night-wind down the vast edges drear
And naked shingles of the world.

Ah, love, let us be true
To one another! for the world, which seems   30
To lie before us like a land of dreams,
So various, so beautiful, so new,
Hath really neither joy, nor love, nor light,
Nor certitude, nor peace, nor help for pain;
And we are here as on a darkling plain
Swept with confused alarms of struggle and flight,
Where ignorant armies clash by night.

A Caution to Poets

WHAT poets feel not, when they make,
    A pleasure in creating,
The world, in *its* turn, will not take
    Pleasure in contemplating.

Palladium

SET where the upper streams of Simois flow
Was the Palladium, high 'mid rock and wood;
And Hector was in Ilium, far below,
And fought, and saw it not, but there it stood.

It stood; and sun and moonshine rain'd their light
On the pure columns of its glen-built hall.
Backward and forward roll'd the waves of fight
Round Troy; but while this stood, Troy could not fall.

73

So, in its lovely moonlight, lives the soul.
Mountains surround it, and sweet virgin air;   10
Cold plashing, past it, crystal waters roll;
We visit it by moments, ah! too rare.

We shall renew the battle in the plain
To-morrow; red with blood will Xanthus be;
Hector and Ajax will be there again;
Helen will come upon the wall to see.

Then 'we shall rust in shade, or shine in strife,
And fluctuate 'twixt blind hopes and blind despairs,
And fancy that we put forth all our life,
And never know how with the soul it fares.   20

Still doth the soul, from its lone fastness high,
Upon our life a ruling effluence send;
And when it fails, fight as we will, we die,
And while it lasts, we cannot wholly end.

Growing Old

WHAT is it to grow old?
Is it to lose the glory of the form,
The lustre of the eye?
Is it for beauty to forgo her wreath?
Yes, but not this alone.

Is it to feel our strength—
Not our bloom only, but our strength—decay?
Is it to feel each limb
Grow stiffer, every function less exact,
Each nerve more loosely strung?   10

Yes, this, and more! but not,
Ah, 'tis not what in youth we dream'd 'twould be!
'Tis not to have our life
Mellow'd and soften'd as with sunset glow,
A golden day's decline!

'Tis not to see the world
As from a height, with rapt prophetic eyes,
And heart profoundly stirr'd;
And weep, and feel the fullness of the past,
The years that are no more!   20

It is to spend long days
And not once feel that we were ever young.
It is to add, immured
In the hot prison of the present, month
To month with weary pain.

It is to suffer this,
And feel but half, and feebly, what we feel.
Deep in our hidden heart
Festers the dull remembrance of a change,
But no emotion—none.   30

It is—last stage of all—
When we are frozen up within, and quite
The phantom of ourselves,
To hear the world applaud the hollow ghost
Which blamed the living man.

The Last Word

CREEP into thy narrow bed,
Creep, and let no more be said!
Vain thy onset! all stands fast;
Thou thyself must break at last.

Let the long contention cease!
Geese are swans, and swans are geese.
Let them have it how they will!
Thou art tired; best be still!

They out-talk'd thee, hiss'd thee, tore thee.
Better men fared thus before thee;   10
Fired their ringing shot and pass'd,
Hotly charged—and sank at last.

Charge once more, then, and be dumb!
Let the victors, when they come,
When the forts of folly fall,
Find thy body by the wall!

Rugby Chapel

NOVEMBER 1857

COLDLY, sadly descends
The autumn evening. The Field
Strewn with its dank yellow drifts

76

Of wither'd leaves, and the elms,
Fade into dimness apace,
Silent;—hardly a shout
From a few boys late at their play!
The lights come out in the street,
In the school-room windows; but cold,
Solemn, unlighted, austere,   10
Through the gathering darkness, arise
The Chapel walls, in whose bound
Thou, my father! art laid.

There thou dost lie, in the gloom
Of the autumn evening. But ah!
That word, *gloom*, to my mind
Brings thee back in the light
Of thy radiant vigour again!
In the gloom of November we pass'd
Days not dark at thy side;   20
Seasons impair'd not the ray
Of thy buoyant cheerfulness clear.
Such thou wast; and I stand
In the autumn evening, and think
Of bygone autumns with thee.

Fifteen years have gone round
Since thou arosest to tread,
In the summer morning, the road
Of death, at a call unforeseen,
Sudden. For fifteen years,   30
We who till then in thy shade
Rested as under the boughs
Of a mighty oak, have endured
Sunshine and rain as we might,
Bare, unshaded, alone,
Lacking the shelter of thee.

O strong soul, by what shore
Tarriest thou now? For that force,
Surely, has not been left vain!
Somewhere, surely, afar,   40
In the sounding labour-house vast
Of being, is practised that strength,
Zealous, beneficent, firm!

Yes, in some far-shining sphere,
Conscious or not of the past,
Still thou performest the word
Of the Spirit in whom thou dost live,
Prompt, unwearied, as here!
Still thou upraisest with zeal
The humble good from the ground,   50
Sternly repressest the bad.
Still, like a trumpet, dost rouse
Those who with half-open eyes
Tread the border-land dim
'Twixt vice and virtue; reviv'st,
Succourest;—this was thy work,
This was thy life upon earth.

What is the course of the life
Of mortal men on the earth?—
Most men eddy about   60
Here and there—eat and drink,
Chatter and love and hate,
Gather and squander, are raised
Aloft, are hurl'd in the dust,
Striving blindly, achieving
Nothing; and, then they die—
Perish; and no one asks
Who or what they have been,
More than he asks what waves

In the moonlit solitudes mild
Of the midmost Ocean, have swell'd,
Foam'd for a moment, and gone.

And there are some, whom a thirst
Ardent, unquenchable, fires,
Not with the crowd to be spent,
Not without aim to go round
In an eddy of purposeless dust,
Effort unmeaning and vain.
Ah yes, some of us strive
Not without action to die
Fruitless, but something to snatch
From dull oblivion, nor all
Glut the devouring grave!
We, we have chosen our path—
Path to a clear-purposed goal,
Path of advance! but it leads
A long, steep journey, through sunk
Gorges, o'er mountains of snow!
Cheerful, with friends, we set forth;
Then, on the height, comes the storm!
Thunder crashes from rock
To rock, the cataracts reply;
Lightnings dazzle our eyes;
Roaring torrents have breach'd
The track, the stream-bed descends
In the place where the wayfarer once
Planted his footstep—the spray
Boils o'er its borders; aloft,
The unseen snow-beds dislodge
Their hanging ruin;—alas,
Havoc is made in our train!
Friends who set forth at our side
Falter, are lost in the storm!

We, we only, are left!
With frowning foreheads, with lips
Sternly compress'd, we strain on,
On—and at nightfall, at last,
Come to the end of our way,
To the lonely inn 'mid the rocks;
Where the gaunt and taciturn Host   110
Stands on the threshold, the wind
Shaking his thin white hairs—
Holds his lantern to scan
Our storm-beat figures, and asks:
Whom in our party we bring?
Whom we have left in the snow?
Sadly we answer: We bring
Only ourselves; we lost
Sight of the rest in the storm.
Hardly ourselves we fought through,   120
Stripp'd, without friends, as we are.
Friends, companions, and train
The avalanche swept from our side.

But thou would'st not *alone*
Be saved, my father! *alone*
Conquer and come to thy goal,
Leaving the rest in the wild.
We were weary, and we
Fearful, and we, in our march,
Fain to drop down and to die.   130
Still thou turnedst, and still
Beckonedst the trembler, and still
Gavest the weary thy hand!
If, in the paths of the world,
Stones might have wounded thy feet,
Toil or dejection have tried
Thy spirit, of that we saw
80

Nothing! to us thou wast still
Cheerful, and helpful, and firm.
Therefore to thee it was given   140
Many to save with thyself;
And, at the end of thy day,
O faithful shepherd! to come,
Bringing thy sheep in thy hand.

And through thee I believe
In the noble and great who are gone;
Pure souls honour'd and blest
By former ages, who else—
Such, so soulless, so poor,
Is the race of men whom I see—   150
Seem'd but a dream of the heart,
Seem'd but a cry of desire.
Yes! I believe that there lived
Others like thee in the past,
Not like the men of the crowd
Who all round me to-day
Bluster or cringe, and make life
Hideous, and arid, and vile;
But souls temper'd with fire,
Fervent, heroic, and good,   160
Helpers and friends of mankind.

Servants of God!—or sons
Shall I not call you? because
Not as servants ye knew
Your Father's innermost mind,
His, who unwillingly sees
One of his little ones lost—
Yours is the praise, if mankind
Hath not as yet in its march
Fainted, and fallen, and died!   170

See! in the rocks of the world
Marches the host of mankind,
A feeble, wavering line.
Where are they tending?—A God
Marshall'd them, gave them their goal.—
Ah, but the way is so long!
Years they have been in the wild!
Sore thirst plagues them; the rocks,
Rising all round, overawe.
Factions divide them; their host   180
Threatens to break, to dissolve.
Ah, keep, keep them combined!
Else, of the myriads who fill
That army, not one shall arrive!
Sole they shall stray; in the rocks
Stagger for ever in vain,
Die one by one in the waste.

Then, in such hour of need
Of your fainting, dispirited race,
Ye, like angels, appear,   190
Radiant with ardour divine.
Beacons of hope, ye appear!
Languor is not in your heart,
Weakness is not in your word,
Weariness not on your brow.

Ye alight in our van; at your voice,
Panic, despair, flee away.
Ye move through the ranks, recall
The stragglers, refresh the outworn,
Praise, re-inspire the brave.   200
Order, courage, return.
Eyes rekindling, and prayers,
Follow your steps as ye go.

Ye fill up the gaps in our files,
Strengthen the wavering line,
Stablish, continue our march,
On, to the bound of the waste,
On, to the City of God.

Stanzas from the Grande Chartreuse

THROUGH Alpine meadows soft-suffused
With rain, where thick the crocus blows,
Past the dark forges long disused,
The mule-track from Saint Laurent goes.
The bridge is cross'd, and slow we ride,
Through forest, up the mountain-side.

The autumnal evening darkens round,
The wind is up, and drives the rain;
While hark! far down, with strangled sound
Doth the Dead Guiers' stream complain,   10
Where that wet smoke among the woods
Over his boiling cauldron broods.

Swift rush the spectral vapours white
Past limestone scars with ragged pines,
Showing—then blotting from our sight.
Halt! through the cloud-drift something shines!
High in the valley, wet and drear,
The huts of Courrerie appear.

Strike leftward! cries our guide; and higher
Mounts up the stony forest-way.   20
At last the encircling trees retire;
Look! through the showery twilight grey
What pointed roofs are these advance?
A palace of the Kings of France?

Approach, for what we seek is here.
Alight and sparely sup and wait
For rest in this outbuilding near;
Then cross the sward and reach that gate;
Knock; pass the wicket! Thou art come
To the Carthusians' world-famed home.   30

The silent courts, where night and day
Into their stone-carved basins cold
The splashing icy fountains play,
The humid corridors behold,
Where ghostlike in the deepening night
Cowl'd forms brush by in gleaming white.

The chapel, where no organ's peal
Invests the stern and naked prayer.
With penitential cries they kneel
And wrestle; rising then, with bare   40
And white uplifted faces stand,
Passing the Host from hand to hand;

Each takes; and then his visage wan
Is buried in his cowl once more.
The cells—the suffering Son of Man
Upon the wall! the knee-worn floor!
And, where they sleep, that wooden bed,
Which shall their coffin be, when dead.

The library, where tract and tome
Not to feed priestly pride are there,   50
To hymn the conquering march of Rome,
Nor yet to amuse, as ours are;
They paint of souls the inner strife,
Their drops of blood, their death in life.

The garden, overgrown—yet mild
Those fragrant herbs are flowering there!
Strong children of the Alpine wild
Whose culture is the brethren's care;
Of human tasks their only one,
And cheerful works beneath the sun.   60

Those halls too, destined to contain
Each its own pilgrim host of old,
From England, Germany, or Spain—
All are before me! I behold
The House, the Brotherhood austere!
And what am I, that I am here?

For rigorous teachers seized my youth,
And purged its faith, and trimm'd its fire,
Show'd me the high white star of Truth,
There bade me gaze, and there aspire;   70
Even now their whispers pierce the gloom:
What dost thou in this living tomb?

Forgive me, masters of the mind!
At whose behest I long ago
So much unlearnt, so much resign'd!
I come not here to be your foe.
I seek these anchorites, not in ruth,
To curse and to deny your truth;

Not as their friend or child I speak!
But as on some far northern strand,   80
Thinking of his own Gods, a Greek
In pity and mournful awe might stand
Before some fallen Runic stone—
For both were faiths, and both are gone.

Wandering between two worlds, one dead,
The other powerless to be born,
With nowhere yet to rest my head,
Like these, on earth I wait forlorn.
Their faith, my tears, the world deride;
I come to shed them at their side.   90

Oh, hide me in your gloom profound,
Ye solemn seats of holy pain!
Take me, cowl'd forms, and fence me round,
Till I possess my soul again!
Till free my thoughts before me roll,
Not chafed by hourly false control.

For the world cries your faith is now
But a dead time's exploded dream;
My melancholy, sciolists say,
Is a pass'd mode, an outworn theme—   100
As if the world had ever had
A faith, or sciolists been sad.

Ah, if it *be* pass'd, take away,
At least, the restlessness—the pain!
Be man henceforth no more a prey
To these out-dated stings again!
The nobleness of grief is gone—
Ah, leave us not the fret alone!

Rome-Sickness

To daily tasks we set our hand,
   And oft the spirit, pent at home,
Breaks out and longs for Switzerland,
   Longs oftener yet and pines for Rome.

I pass'd to-day o'er Walton Heath—
   The coming spring-time's earliest stir
Quickened and moved, a happy breath,
   In moss, and gorse, and shining fir.

Fortunate firs who never think
   How firs less curst by Fortune's frown   10
O'er Glion fringe the mountain's brink,
   Or dot the slopes to Vevey down.

I cross'd St. George's Hill to-day—
   There in the leaf-strewn copse I found
The tender foxglove-plants display
   Their first green muffle on the ground.

They envy not, this tranquil brood,
   The cyclamens whose blossoms fill
With fragrance all Frascati's wood
   Along the gracious Alban Hill!   20

Man only, with eternal bent
   To come and go, to shift and range,
At life and living not content,
   Chafes in his place, and pines for change.

Yet happy—since his feverish blood
   Leaves him no rest, and change he will—
When restlessness is restless good,
   Still mending, lessening, human ill!

Unwearied, as from land to land
   The incessant warrior takes his way,   30
To hold the light and reach the hand
   To all who sink, to all who stray!

S.S. Lusitania

I READ in Dante how that horned light,
Which hid Ulysses, waved itself and said:
'Following the sun, we set our vessel's head
To the great main; pass'd Seville on the right

'And Ceuta on the left; then southward sped.
At last in air, far off, dim rose a Height.
We cheer'd; but from it rush'd a blast of might,
And struck—and o'er us the sea-waters spread.'

I dropped the book, and of my child I thought
In his long black ship speeding night and day   10
O'er those same seas; dark Teneriffe, rose fraught

With omen, 'Oh! were that Mount pass'd', I say.
Then the door opens and this card is brought:
'Reach'd Cape Verde Islands, "Lusitania".'

PART TWO

Prose

Teachers and Inspectors

The true duty of an Inspector towards your Lordships, the truest kindness towards the managers and teachers of schools, seems to me to be this—that the Inspector, keeping his eye above all upon the most tangible and cognizable among those details into which he is directed to inquire, and omitting, as much as possible, the consideration of what is not positive and palpable, should construct a plain matter-of-fact report upon each school which he visits, and should place it, without suppression, before your Lordships. But, although I thus press for the most un-varnished and literal report on their schools, I can assure the teachers of them that it is from no harshness or want of sympathy towards them that I do so. No one feels more than I do how laborious is their work, how trying at times to the health and spirits, how full of difficulty even for the best; how much fuller for those, whom I too often see attempting the work of a schoolmaster—men of weak health and purely studious habits, who betake themselves to this profession, as affording the means to continue their favourite pursuits: not knowing, alas, that for all but men of the most singular and exceptional vigour and energy, there are no pursuits more irreconcilable than those of the student and of the schoolmaster. Still, the quantity of work actually done at present by teachers is immense: the sincerity and devotedness of much of it is even affecting. They themselves will be the greatest gainers by a system of reporting which clearly states what they do and what they fail to do; not one which drowns alike success and failure, the able and the inefficient, in a common flood of vague approbation.

1854

Schools that Civilize

Nowhere are good school-buildings, and, above all, a good playground, such a potent means of attraction to scholars as in London: for nowhere are the benefits of air, light, space, and free means of exercise, so scantily possessed by them in their homes. The spacious playgrounds attached to the Wesleyan practising schools in Westminster, in the midst of a densely crowded and poverty-stricken locality, form, in my opinion, one of the most delightful features of that institution; and form also one of its best agents in the work of humanizing and civilizing the neighbourhood in which it is placed.

1855

English for the English

I found in the French schools good manuals for teaching special subjects—a good manual for teaching arithmetic, a good manual for teaching grammar, a good manual for teaching geography; what was wanting there, as it is wanting with us, was a good *reading-book*, or course of reading-books. It is not enough remembered in how many cases his reading-book forms the whole literature, except his Bible, of the child attending a primary school. If then, instead of literature, his reading-book, as is too often the case, presents him with a jejune encyclopaedia of positive information, the result is that he has, except his Bible, no literature, no *humanizing* instruction at all. If, again, his reading-book, as is also too often the case, presents him with bad literature instead of good—with the writing of second or third-rate authors, feeble, incorrect, and colourless—he has not, as the rich have, the corrective of an abundance of good literature to counteract the bad effect of trivial and ill-written school-books; the second- or third-rate literature of his school-book remains for him his sole, or, at least, his principal literary standard. Dry scientific disquisitions, and literary compositions of an inferior order, are indeed the worst possible instruments for teaching children to read well. But besides the fault of not fulfilling this, their essential function, the ill-compiled reading-books I speak of have, I say, for the poor scholar, the graver fault of actually doing what they can to spoil his taste, when they are nearly his only means for forming it. I have seen school-books belonging to the cheapest, and therefore most popular series in use in our primary schools, in which far more than half of the poetical extracts were the composition either of the anonymous compilers themselves, or of American writers of the second and third order; and these books were to be some poor child's Anthology of a literature so varied and so powerful as the English! To this defectiveness of our reading-books I attribute much of that grave and discouraging deficiency in anything like literary taste and feeling, which even well-instructed pupil-teachers of four or five years' training, which even the ablest students in our training schools, still continue almost invariably to exhibit; a deficiency, to remedy which, the progressive development of our school system, and the very considerable increase of information among the people, appear to avail little or nothing. I believe that nothing would so much contribute to remedy it as the diffusion in our elementary schools of reading-books of which the contents were really well selected and interesting. Such lessons would be far better adapted than a treatise on the atmosphere, the steam-engine, or the pump, to attain the proper end of a reading-book, that of teaching scholars to read well; they would also afford the best chance of inspiring quick scholars with a real love for reading and literature in the only way in which such a love is ever really inspired, by animating and moving them; and if they succeeded in doing this, they would have this further advantage, that the literature for which they inspired a taste would be a good, a sound, and a truly refining literature; not a literature such as that of most of the few attractive pieces in our current reading-books, a literature over which no cultivated person would dream of wasting his time.

1860

Examinations (1)

I have been struck by one result of the practical working of the new examinations which I am sure your Lordships never intended. I mean the peculiar severity with which they tell upon the younger classes in a school owing to the timidity natural to this age. When a boy of eleven or twelve years of age is so shy that he cannot open his mouth before a stranger, one may without harshness say that he ought to have been taught better and refuse him his grant; but when a child of seven is in this predicament one can hardly, without harshness, say the same thing, and to refuse him his grant for a timidity which is not, in his case, a school fault, seems to be going beyond the intention of your Lordships, who designed the refusal of your grants to be a punishment for school faults.

1863

Examinations (2)

All test examinations . . . may be said to narrow reading upon a certain given point, and to make it mechanical. If a man wants a certificate or diploma of you, you say you will give it him if he learns this and that, which you prescribe; and you may be said to cramp his studies by thus limiting them. Certainly, if a man wants a certificate, or a diploma, or honours, of you, you must fix just what he shall get them for, which is by no means of the same extent as a liberal education. But this is a reason against turning too much of a man's reading into reading for certificates, diplomas, or honours. That is why our University system of examinations, competitions, and honours, is so little favoured in Germany. But, at any rate, to make a narrowing system of test examinations govern the whole inspection of our primary schools, when we have before us, not individuals wanting a diploma from us, but organizations wanting to be guided by us into the best ways of learning and teaching, seems like saddling ourselves with a confessed cause of imperfection unnecessarily.

Admitting the stimulus of the test examination to be salutary, we may therefore yet say that when it is over-employed it has two faults: it tends to make the instruction mechanical, and to set a bar to duly extending it. School grants earned in the way fixed by the Revised Code—by the scholar performing a certain *minimum* expressly laid down beforehand—must inevitably concentrate the teacher's attention on the means for producing this *minimum*, and not simply on the good instruction of the school. The danger to be guarded against is the mistake of treating these two—the producing this *minimum* successfully and the good instruction of the school—as if they were identical. The safeguard seems to be in reducing the overwhelming preponderance of this examination and its result, at the same time that we retain all its useful stimulus.   1869

Examinations (3)

More free play for the Inspector, and more free play, in consequence, for the teacher, is what is wanted. . . . In the game of mechanical contrivances the teachers will in the end beat us; and as it now found possible, by ingenious preparation, to get children through the Revised Code examination in reading, writing, and ciphering, without their really knowing how to read, write, or cipher, so it will with practice, no doubt, be found possible to get the three-fourths of the one-fifth of the children over six through the examination in grammar, geography, and history, without their really knowing any one of these three matters.

1867

The Standard of Life

. . . More and more pressure there will be, especially in the instruction of the children of the working classes, whose time for schooling is short, to substitute natural science for literature and history as the more useful alternative. And what a curious state of things it would be if every scholar who had passed through the course of our primary schools knew that, when a taper burns, the wax is converted into carbonic acid and water, and thought, at the same time, that a good paraphrase for *Canst thou not minister to a mind diseased*, was, *Can you not wait upon the lunatic!* The problem to be solved is a great deal more complicated than many of the friends of natural science suppose.

They see clearly enough, for instance, how the working classes are, in their ignorance, constantly violating the laws of health, and suffering accordingly and they look to a spread of sound natural science as the remedy. What they do not see is that to know the laws of health ever so exactly, as a mere piece of positive knowledge, will carry a man in general no great way. To have the power of using, which is the thing wished, these data of natural science, a man must, in general, have first been in some measure *moralised*; and for moralising him it will be found not easy, I think, to dispense with those old agents, letters, poetry, religion. So let not our teachers be led to imagine, whatever they may hear and see of the call for natural science, that their literary cultivation is unimportant. The fruitful use of natural science itself depends, in a very great degree, on having effected in the whole man, by means of letters, a rise in what the political economists call *the standard of life*.

1876

Creative Activity

Of such high importance, in relieving the strain of mental effort, is the sense of pleasurable activity and of creation. Of course a great deal of the work in elementary schools must necessarily be of a mechanical kind. But whatever introduces any sort of creative activity to relieve the passive reception of knowledge is valuable. The kindergarten exercises are useful for this reason, the management of tools is useful, singing is useful. The poetry exercise, if properly managed, is of great use, and this way I have always been in favour of it. . . . People talk contemptuously of 'learning lines by heart'; but if the child is brought, as he easily can be brought, to *throw himself into* a piece of poetry, an exercise of creative activity has been set up in him quite different from the effort of learning a list of words to spell, or a list of flesh-making and heat-giving foods, or a list of capes and bays, or a list of reigns and battles, and capable of greatly relieving the strain from learning these and of affording a lively pleasure. It is true, language, and geography, and history, and the elements of natural science are all capable of being taught in a less mechanical and more interesting manner than that in which they are commonly taught now; they may be so taught as to call forth pleasurable activity in the pupil. But those disciplines are equally valuable which call this activity forth most surely and directly.

1882

Democracy

. . . It is because aristocracies almost inevitably fail to appreciate justly, or even to take into their mind, the instinct pushing the masses towards expansion and fuller life, that they lose their hold over them. It is the old story of the incapacity of aristocracies for ideas—the secret of their want of success in modern epochs. The people treats them with flagrant injustice, when it denies all obligation to them. They can, and often do, impart a high spirit, a fine ideal of grandeur, to the people; thus they lay the foundations of a great nation. But they leave the people still the multitude, the crowd; they have small belief in the power of the ideas which are its life. Themselves a power reposing on all which is most solid, material, and visible, they are slow to attach any great importance to influences impalpable, spiritual, and viewless. Although, therefore, a disinterested looker-on might often be disposed, seeing what has actually been achieved by aristocracies, to wish to retain or replace them in their preponderance, rather than commit a nation to the hazards of a new and untried future; yet the masses instinctively feel that they can never consent to this without renouncing the inmost impulse of their being; and that they should make such a renunciation

98

cannot seriously be expected of them. Except on conditions which make its expansion, in the sense understood by itself, fully possible, democracy will never frankly ally itself with aristocracy; and on these conditions perhaps no aristocracy will ever frankly ally itself with it. Even the English aristocracy, so politic, so capable of compromises, has shown no signs of being able so to transform itself as to render such an alliance possible. The reception given by the Peers to the bill for establishing life-peerages was, in this respect, of ill omen. The separation between aristocracy and democracy will probably, therefore, go on still widening.

And it must in fairness be added, that as in one most important part of general human culture,—openness to ideas and ardour for them,—aristocracy is less advanced than democracy, to replace or keep the latter under the tutelage of the former would in some respects be actually unfavourable to the progress of the world. At epochs when new ideas are powerfully fermenting in a society, and profoundly changing its spirit, aristocracies, as they are in general not long suffered to guide it without question, so are they by nature not well fitted to guide it intelligently.

In England, democracy has been slow in developing itself, having met with much to withstand it, not only in the worth of the aristocracy, but also in the fine qualities of the common people. The aristocracy has been more in sympathy with the common people than perhaps any other aristocracy. It has rarely given them great umbrage; it has neither been frivolous, so as to provoke their contempt, nor impertinent, so as to provoke their irritation. Above all, it has in general meant to act with justice, according to its own notions of justice. Therefore the feeling of admiring deference to such a class was more deep-rooted in the people of this country, more cordial, and more persistent, than in any people of the Continent. But, besides this, the vigour and high spirit of the English common people bred in them a self-reliance which disposed each man to act individually and inde-pendently; and so long as this disposition prevails through a nation divided into classes, the predominance of an aristocracy, of the class containing the greatest and strongest individuals of the nation, is secure. Democracy is a force in which the concert of a great number of men makes up for the weakness of each man taken by himself; democracy accepts a certain relative rise in their condition, obtainable by this concert for a great number, as something desirable in itself, because though this is undoubtedly far below grandeur, it is yet a good deal above insignificance. A very strong, self-reliant people neither easily learns to act in concert, nor easily brings itself to regard any middling good, any good short of the best, as an object ardently to be coveted and striven for. It keeps its eye on the grand prizes, and these are to be won only by distancing competitors, by getting before one's comrades, by succeeding all by one's self; and so long as a people works thus individually, it does not work democratically. The English people has all the qualities which dispose a people to work individually; may it never lose them! A people without the salt of these qualities, relying wholly on mutual co-operation, and proposing to itself second-rate ideals, would arrive at the pettiness and stationariness of China. But the English people is no longer so entirely ruled by them as not to show visible beginnings of democratic action; it becomes more and more sensible to the irresistible seduction of democratic ideas, promising to each individual of the multitude increased self-respect and expansion with the increased importance and authority of the multitude to which he belongs, with the diminished preponderance of the aristocratic class above him.

While the habit and disposition of deference are thus dying out among the lower classes of the English nation, it seems to me indisputable that the advantages which command deference, that eminent superiority in high feeling, dignity, and culture, tend to diminish among the highest class. I shall not be suspected of any inclination to underrate the aristocracy of this country. I regard it as the worthiest, as it certainly has been the most successful, aristocracy of which history makes record. If it has not been able to develop excellences which do not belong to the nature of an aristocracy, yet it has been able to avoid defects to which the nature of an aristocracy is peculiarly prone. But I cannot read the history of the flowering time of the English aristocracy, the eighteenth century, and then look at this aristocracy in our own century, without feeling that there has been a change. I am not now thinking of private and domestic virtues, of morality, of decorum. Perhaps with respect to these there has in this class, as in society at large, been a change for the better. I am thinking of those public and conspicuous virtues by which the multitude is captivated and led,—lofty spirit, commanding character, exquisite culture. It is true that the advance of all classes in culture and refinement may make the culture of one class, which, isolated, appeared remarkable, appear so no longer; but exquisite culture and great dignity are always something rare and striking, and it is the distinction of the English aristocracy, in the eighteenth century, that not only was their culture something rare by comparison with the rawness of the masses, it was something rare and admirable in itself. It is rather that this rare culture of the highest class has actually somewhat declined, than that it has come to look less by juxta-position with the augmented culture of other classes. . . .

The great middle classes of this country are conscious of no weakness, no inferiority; they do not want any one to provide anything for them. Such as they are, they believe that the freedom and prosperity of England are their work, and that the future belongs to them. No one esteems them more than I do; but those who esteem them most, and who most believe in their capabilities, can render them no better service than by pointing out in what they underrate their deficiencies, and how their deficiencies, if unremedied, may impair their future. They want culture and dignity; they want ideas. Aristocracy has culture and dignity; democracy has readiness for new ideas, and ardour for what ideas it possesses. Of these, our middle class has the last only; ardour for the ideas it already possesses. It believes ardently in liberty, it believes ardently in industry; and, by its zealous belief in these two ideas, it has accomplished great things. What it has accomplished by its belief in industry is patent to all the world. The liberties of England are less exclusive work than it supposes; for these, aristocracy has achieved nearly as much. Still, of one inestimable part of liberty, liberty of thought, the middle class has been (without precisely intending it) the principal champion. The intellectual action of the Church of England upon the nation has been insignificant; its social action has been great. The social action of Protestant Dissent, that genuine product of the English middle class, has not been civilising; its positive intellectual action has been insignificant; its negative intellectual action,—in so far as by strenuously maintaining for itself, against persecution, liberty of conscience and the right of free opinion, it at the same time maintained and established this right as a universal principle,—has been invaluable. But the actual results of this negative intellectual service rendered by Protestant Dissent,—by the middle class,—to the whole community, great as they undoubtedly are, must not be taken for something which they are not. It is a very great thing to be able to think as you like; but, after all, an important question remains: *what* you think. It is a fine thing to secure a free stage and no favour; but, after all, the part which you play on that stage will have to be criticized. Now, all the liberty and industry in the world will not ensure these two things: a high reason and a fine culture. They may favour them, but they will not of themselves produce them; they may exist without them. But it is by the appearance of these two things, in some shape or other, in the life of a nation, that it becomes something more than an independent, an energetic, a successful nation,—that it becomes a *great* nation.

In modern epochs the part of a high reason, of ideas, acquires constantly increasing importance in the conduct of the world's affairs. A fine culture is the complement of a high reason, and it is in the conjunction of both with character, with energy, that the ideal for men and nations is to be placed. It is common to hear remarks on the frequent divorce between culture and character, and to infer from this that culture is a mere varnish, and that character only deserves any serious attention. No error can be more fatal. Culture without character is, no doubt, something frivolous, vain, and weak; but character without culture is, on the other hand, something raw, blind, and dangerous. The most interesting, the most truly glorious peoples, are those in which the alliance of the two has been effected most successfully, and its result spread most widely. This is why the spectacle of ancient Athens has such profound interest for a rational man; that is the spectacle of the culture of a *people*. It is not an aristocracy, leavening with its own high spirit the multitude which it wields, but leaving it the unformed multitude still; it is not a democracy, acute and energetic, but tasteless, narrow-minded, and ignoble; it is the middle and lower classes in the highest development of their humanity that these classes have yet reached. It was the *many* who relished those arts, who were not satisfied with less than those monuments. In the conversations recorded by Plato, or even by the matter-of-fact Xenophon, which for the free yet refined discussion of ideas have set the tone for the whole cultivated world, shopkeepers and tradesmen of Athens mingle as speakers. For any one but a pedant, this is why a handful of Athenians of two thousand years ago are more interesting than the millions of most nations our contemporaries. Surely, if they knew this, those friends of progress, who have confidently pronounced the remains of the ancient world to be so much lumber, and a classical education an aristocratic impertinence, might be inclined to reconsider their sentence.

The course taken in the next fifty years by the middle classes of this nation will probably give a decisive turn to its history. If they will not seek the alliance of the State for their own elevation, if they go on exaggerating their spirit of individualism, if they persist in their jealousy of all governmental action, if they cannot learn that the antipathies and the shibboleths of a past age are now an anachronism for them—that will not prevent them, probably, from getting the rule of their country for a season, but they will certainly *Americanize* it. They will rule it by their energy, but they will deteriorate it by their low ideals and want of culture. In the decline of the aristocratical element, which in some sort supplied an ideal to ennoble the spirit of the nation and to keep it together, there will be no other element present to perform this service. It is of itself a serious calamity for a nation that its tone of feeling and grandeur of spirit should be lowered or dulled. But the calamity appears far more serious still when we consider that the middle classes, remaining as they are now, with their narrow, harsh, unintelligent, and unattractive spirit and culture, will almost certainly fail to mould or assimilate the masses below them, whose sympathies are at the present moment actually wider and more liberal than theirs. They arrive, these masses, eager to enter into possession of the world, to gain a more vivid sense of their own life and activity. In this their irrepressible development, their natural educators and initiators are those immediately above them, the middle classes. If these classes cannot win their sympathy or give them their direction, society is in danger of falling into anarchy.

Therefore, with all the force I can, I wish to urge upon the middle classes of this country, both that they might be very greatly profited by the action of the State, and also that they are continuing their opposition to such action out of an unfounded fear. But at the same time I say that the middle classes have the right, in admitting the action of government, to make the condition that this government shall be one of their own adoption, one that they can trust. To ensure this is now in their own power. If they do not as yet ensure this, they ought to do so, they have the means of doing so. Two centuries ago they had not; now they have. Having this security, let them now show themselves jealous to keep the action of the State equitable and rational, rather than to exclude the action of the State altogether. If the State acts amiss, let them check it, but let them no longer take it for granted that the State cannot possibly act usefully.

from *The Popular Education of France*

The Function of Criticism

. . . The Englishman has been called a political animal, and he values what is political and practical so much that ideas easily become objects of dislike in his eyes, and thinkers 'miscreants', because ideas and thinkers have rashly meddled with politics and practice. This would be all very well if the dislike and neglect confined themselves to ideas transported out of their own sphere, and meddling rashly with practice; but they are inevitably extended to ideas as such, and to the whole life of intelligence; practice is everything, a free play of the mind is nothing. The notion of the free play of the mind upon all subjects being a pleasure in itself, being an object of desire, being an essential provider of elements without which a nation's spirit, whatever compensations it may have for them, must, in the long run, die of inanition, hardly enters into an Englishman's thoughts. It is noticeable that the word *curiosity*, which in other languages is used in a good sense, to mean, as a high and fine quality of man's nature, just this disinterested love of a free play of the mind on all subjects, for its own sake,—it is noticeable, I say, that this word has in our language no sense of the kind, no sense but a rather bad and disparaging one. But criticism, real criticism, is essentially the exercise of this very quality; it obeys an instinct prompting it to try to know the best that is known and thought in the world, irrespectively of practice, politics, and everything of the kind; and to value knowledge and thought as they approach this best, without the intrusion of any other considerations whatever. This is an instinct for which there is, I think, little original sympathy in the practical English nature, and what there was of it has undergone a long benumbing period of check and suppression in the epoch of concentration which followed the French Revolution.

But epochs of concentration cannot well endure for ever; epochs of expansion, in the due course of things, follow them. Such an epoch of expansion seems to be opening in this country. In the first place all danger of a hostile forcible pressure of foreign ideas upon our practice has long disappeared; like the traveller in the fable, therefore, we begin to wear our cloak a little more loosely. Then, with a long peace the ideas of Europe steal gradually and amicably in, and mingle, though in infinitesimally small quantities at a time, with our own notions. Then, too, in spite of all that is said about the absorbing and brutalizing influence of our passionate material progress, it seems to me indisputable that this progress is likely, though not certain, to lead in the end to an apparition of intellectual life; and that man, after he has made himself perfectly comfortable and has now to determine what to do with himself next, may begin to remember that he has a mind, and that the mind may be made the source of great pleasure. I grant it is mainly the privilege of faith, at present, to discern this end to our railways, our business, and our fortune-making; but we shall see if, here as elsewhere, faith is not in the end the true prophet. Our ease, our travelling, and our unbounded liberty to hold just as hard and securely as we please to the practice to which our notions have given birth, all tend to beget an inclination to deal a little more freely with these notions themselves, to canvass them a little, to penetrate a little into their real nature. Flutterings of curiosity, in the foreign sense of the word, appear amongst us, and it is in these that criticism must look to find its account. Criticism first; a time of true creative activity, perhaps,—which, as I have said, must inevitably be preceded amongst us by a time of criticism,— hereafter, when criticism has done its work.

It is of the last importance that English criticism should clearly discern what rules for its course, in order to avail itself of the field now opening to it, and to produce fruit for the future, it ought to take. The rules may be given in one word; by being *disinterested*. And how is it to be disinterested? By keeping aloof from practice; by resolutely following the law of its own nature, which is to be a free play of the mind on all subjects which it touches; by steadily refusing to lend itself to any of these ulterior, political, practical considerations about ideas, which plenty of people will be sure to attach to them, which perhaps ought often to be attached to them, which in this country at any rate are certain to be attached to them quite sufficiently, but which criticism has really nothing to do with. Its business is, as I have said, simply to know the best that is known and thought in the world, and by in its turn making this known, to create a current of true and fresh ideas. Its business is to do this with inflexible honesty, with due ability; but its business is to do no more, and to leave alone all questions of practical consequences and applications, questions which will never fail to have due prominence given to them. Else criticism, besides being really false to its own nature, merely continues in the old rut which it has hitherto followed in this country, and will certainly miss the chance now given to it. For what is at present the bane of criticism in this country? It is that practical considerations cling to it and stifle it; it subserves interests not its own; our organs of criticism are organs of men and parties having practical ends to serve, and with them those practical ends are the first thing and the play of mind the second; so much play of mind as is compatible with the prosecution of those practical ends is all that is wanted. An organ like the *Revue des Deux Mondes*, having for its main function to understand and utter the best that is known and thought in the world, existing, it may be said, as just an organ for a free play of the mind, we have not; but we have the *Edinburgh Review*, existing as an organ of the old Whigs, and for as much play of the mind as may suit its being that; we have the *Quarterly Review*,

107

existing as an organ of the Tories, and for as much play of mind as may suit its being that; we have the *British Quarterly Review*, existing as an organ of the political Dissenters, and for as much play of mind as may suit its being that; we have the *Times*, existing as an organ of the common, satisfied, well-to-do Englishman, and for as much play of mind as may suit its being that. And so on through all the various factions, political and religious, of our society; every faction has, as such, its organ of criticism, but the notion of combining all factions in the common pleasure of a free disinterested play of mind meets with no favour. Directly this play of mind wants to have more scope, and to forget the pressure of practical considerations a little, it is checked, it is made to feel the chain. We saw this the other day in the extinction, so much to be regretted, of the *Home and Foreign Review*; perhaps in no organ of criticism in this country was there so much knowledge, so much play of mind; but these could not save it. The *Dublin Review* subordinates play of mind to the practical business of Roman Catholicism, and lives. It must needs be that men should act in sects and parties, that each of these sects and parties should have its organ, and should make this organ subserve the interests of its action; but it would be well, too, that there should be a criticism, not the minister of these interests, not their enemy, but absolutely and entirely independent of them. No other criticism will ever attain any real authority or make any real way towards its end,—the creating a current of true and fresh ideas.

It is because criticism has so little kept in the pure intellectual sphere, has so little detached itself from practice, has been so directly polemical and controversial, that it has so ill accomplished, in this country, its best spiritual work; which is to keep man from a self-satisfaction which is retarding and vulgarizing, to lead him towards perfection, by making his mind dwell upon what is excellent in itself, and the absolute beauty and fitness of things. . . .

It will be said that it is a very subtle and indirect action which

I am thus prescribing for criticism, and that, by embracing in this manner the Indian virtue of detachment and abandoning the sphere of practical life, it condemns itself to a slow and obscure work. Slow and obscure it may be, but it is the only proper work of criticism. The mass of mankind will never have any ardent zeal for seeing things as they are; very inadequate ideas will always satisfy them. On these inadequate ideas reposes, and must repose, the general practice of the world. That is as much as saying that whoever sets himself to see things as they are will find himself one of a very small circle; but it is only by this small circle resolutely doing its own work that adequate ideas will ever get current at all. The rush and roar of practical life will always have a dizzying and attracting effect upon the most collected spectator, and tend to draw him into its vortex; most of all will this be the case where that life is so powerful as it is in England. But it is only by remaining collected, and refusing to lend himself to the point of view of the practical man, that the critic can do the practical man any service; and it is only by the greatest sincerity in pursuing his own course, and by at last convincing even the practical man of his sincerity, that he can escape misunderstandings which perpetually threaten him.

For the practical man is not apt for fine distinctions, and yet in these distinctions truth and the highest culture greatly find their account. But it is not easy to lead a practical man,—unless you reassure him as to your practical intentions, you have no chance of leading him,—to see that a thing which he has always been used to look at from one side only, which he greatly values, and which, looked at from that side, more than deserves, perhaps, all the prizing and admiring which he bestows upon it, —that this thing, looked at from another side, may appear much less beneficent and beautiful, and yet retain all its claims to our practical allegiance. Where shall we find language innocent enough, how shall we make the spotless purity of our intentions evident enough, to enable us to say to the political Englishman that the British constitution itself, which, seen from the practical side, looks such a magnificent organ of progress and virtue, seen from the speculative side,—with its compromises, its love of facts, its horror of theory, its studied avoidance of clear thoughts,—that, seen from this side, our august constitution sometimes looks,—forgive me, shade of Lord Somers!—a colossal machine for the manufacture of Philistines? . . .

Criticism must maintain its independence of the practical spirit and its aims. Even with well-meant efforts of the practical spirit it must express dissatisfaction, if in the sphere of the ideal they seem impoverishing and limiting. It must not hurry on to the goal because of its practical importance. It must be patient, and know how to wait; and flexible, and know how to attach itself to things and how to withdraw from them. It must be apt to study and praise elements that for the fulness of spiritual perfection are wanted, even though they belong to a power which in the practical sphere may be maleficent. It must be apt to discern the spiritual shortcomings or illusions of powers that in the practical sphere may be beneficent. And this without any notion of favouring or injuring, in the practical sphere, one power or the other; without any notion of playing off, in this sphere, one power against the other. When one looks, for instance, at the English Divorce Court,—an institution which perhaps has its practical conveniences, but which in the ideal sphere is so hideous; an institution which neither makes divorce impossible nor makes it decent, which allows a man to get rid of his wife, or a wife of her husband, but makes them drag one another first, for the public edification, through a mire of unutterable infamy,—when one looks at this charming institution, I say, with its crowded trials, its newspaper reports, and its money compensations, this institution in which the gross unregenerate British Philistine has indeed stamped an image of himself,—one may be permitted to find the marriage theory of Catholicism refreshing and elevating. Or when Protestantism, in virtue of its supposed rational and intellectual origin, gives the law to criticism too magisterially, criticism may and must remind it that its pretensions, in this respect, are illusive and do it harm; that the Reformation was a moral rather than an intellectual event; that Luther's theory of grace no more exactly reflects the mind of the spirit than Bossuet's philosophy of history reflects it; and that there is no more antecedent probability of the Bishop of Durham's stock of ideas being agreeable to perfect reason than of Pope Pius the Ninth's. But criticism will not on that account forget the achievements of Protestantism in the practical and moral sphere; nor that, even in the intellectual sphere, Protestantism, though in a blind and stumbling manner, carried forward the Renaissance, while Catholicism threw itself violently across its path.

I lately heard a man of thought and energy contrasting the want of ardour and movement which he now found amongst young men in this country with what he remembered in his own youth, twenty years ago. 'What reformers we were then!' he exclaimed; 'what a zeal we had! how we canvassed every institution in Church and State, and were prepared to remodel them all on first principles!' He was inclined to regret, as a spiritual flagging, the lull which he saw. I am disposed rather to regard it as a pause in which the turn to a new mode of spiritual progress is being accomplished. Everything was long seen, by the young and ardent among us, in inseparable connection with politics and practical life. We have pretty well exhausted the benefits of seeing things in this connection, we have got all that can be got by so seeing them. Let us try a more disinterested mode of seeing them; let us betake ourselves more to the serener life of the mind and spirit. This life, too, may have its excesses and dangers; but they are not for us at present. Let us think of quietly enlarging our stock of true and fresh ideas, and not, as soon as we get an idea or half an idea, be running out with it into the street, and trying to make it rule there. Our ideas will, in the end, shape the world all the better for maturing a little. Perhaps in fifty years' time it will in the English House of Commons be an objection to an institution that it is an anomaly, and my friend the Member of Parliament will shudder in his grave. But let us in the meanwhile rather endeavour that in twenty years' time it may, in English literature, be an objection to a proposition that it is absurd. That will be a change so vast, that the imagination almost fails to grasp it. *Ab integro saeclorum nascitur ordo.*[1]

If I have insisted so much on the course which criticism must take where politics and religion are concerned, it is because, where these burning matters are in question, it is most likely to go astray. In general, its course is determined for it by the idea which is the law of its being; the idea of a disinterested endeavour to learn and propagate the best that is known and thought in the world, and thus to establish a current of fresh and true ideas. By the very nature of things, as England is not all the world, much of the best that is known and thought in the world cannot be of English growth, must be foreign; by the nature of things, again, it is just this that we are least likely to know, while English thought is streaming in upon us from all sides, and takes excellent care that we shall not be ignorant of its existence; the English critic, therefore, must dwell much on foreign thought, and with particular heed on any part of it, which, while significant and fruitful in itself, is for any reason specially likely to escape him. Judging is often spoken of as the critic's one business, and so in some sense it is; but the judgment which almost insensibly forms itself in a fair and clear mind, along with fresh knowledge, is the valuable one; and thus knowledge, and ever fresh knowledge, must be the critic's great concern for himself; and it is by communicating fresh knowledge, and letting his own judgment pass along with it,—but insensibly, and in the second place, not the first, as a sort of companion and clue, not as an abstract lawgiver,—that he will generally do most good to his readers. Sometimes, no doubt, for the sake of establishing an author's place in literature, and his relation to a central standard (and if this is not done, how are we to get at our *best in the world?*)

[1] The cycle of the centuries is born afresh.

criticism may have to deal with a subject-matter so familiar that fresh knowledge is out of the question, and then it must be all judgment; an enunciation and detailed application of principles. Here the great safeguard is never to let oneself become abstract, always to retain an intimate and lively consciousness of the truth of what one is saying, and, the moment this fails us, to be sure that something is wrong. Still, under all circumstances, this mere judgment and application of principles is, in itself, not the most satisfactory work to the critic; like mathematics, it is tautological, and cannot well give us, like fresh learning, the sense of creative activity. To have this sense is, as I said at the beginning, the great happiness and the great proof of being alive, and it is not denied to criticism to have it; but then criticism must be sincere, simple, flexible, ardent, ever widening its knowledge. Then it may have, in no contemptible measure, a joyful sense of creative activity; a sense which a man of insight and conscience will prefer to what he might derive from a poor, starved, fragmentary, inadequate creation. And at some epochs no other creation is possible.

Still, in full measure, the sense of creative activity belongs only to genuine creation; in literature we must never forget that. But what true man of letters can ever forget it? It is no such common matter for a gifted nature to come into possession of a current of true and living ideas, and to produce amidst the inspiration of them, that we are likely to underrate it. The epochs of Æschylus and Shakespeare make us feel their pre-eminence. In an epoch like those is, no doubt, the true life of literature; there is the promised land, towards which criticism can only beckon. That promised land it will not be ours to enter, and we shall die in the wilderness: but to have desired to enter it, to have saluted it from afar, is already, perhaps, the best distinction among contemporaries; it will certainly be the best title to esteem with posterity.

Essays in Criticism, First Series

The Modern Spirit

In making out the case for recognizing the importance of Heine (the German poet, 1797-1856) Arnold contends that Goethe, and then Heine, did much to free Europe from its 'old doctrine'. The general statement below is included here because it is an excellent clarification of Arnold's views on the need for change.

Modern times find themselves with an immense system of institutions, established facts, accredited dogmas, customs, rules, which have come to them from times not modern. In this system their life has to be carried forward; yet they have a sense that this system is not of their own creation, that it by no means corresponds exactly with the wants of their actual life, that, for them, it is customary, not rational. The awakening of this sense is the awakening of the modern spirit. The modern spirit is now awake almost everywhere; the sense of want of correspondence between the forms of modern Europe and its spirit, between the new wine of the eighteenth and nineteenth centuries, and the old bottles of the eleventh and twelfth centuries, or even of the sixteenth and seventeenth, almost everyone now perceives; it is no longer dangerous to affirm that this want of correspondence exists; people are even beginning to be shy of defending it. To remove this want of correspondence is beginning to be the settled endeavour of most persons of good sense. Dissolvents of the old European system of dominant ideas and facts we must all be, all of us who have any power of working; what we have to study is that we may not be acrid dissolvents of it.

from 'Heinrich Heine' in *Essays in Criticism*, First Series

On Translating Homer

. . . Pope's movement, however, though rapid, is not of the same kind as Homer's; and here I come to the real objection to rhyme in a translation of Homer. It is commonly said that rhyme is to be abandoned in a translation of Homer, because 'the exigencies of rhyme', to quote Mr Newman, 'positively forbid faithfulness'; because 'a just translation of any ancient poet in rhyme', to quote Cowper, 'is impossible'. This, however, is merely an accidental objection to rhyme. If this were all, it might be supposed that if rhymes were more abundant Homer could be adequately translated in rhyme. But this is not so; there is a deeper, a substantial objection to rhyme in a translation of Homer. It is, that rhyme inevitably tends to pair lines which in the original are independent, and thus the movement of the poem is changed. In these lines of Chapman, for instance, from Sarpedon's speech to Glaucus, in the twelfth book of the *Iliad:*

> O friend, if keeping back
> Would keep back age from us, and death, and that we might not wrack
> In this life's human sea at all, but that deferring now
> We shunned death ever,—nor would I half this vain valor show,
> Nor glorify a folly so, to wish thee to advance;
> But since we *must* go, though not here, and that besides the chance
> Proposed now, there are infinite fates, etc.

Here the necessity of making the line,

> Nor glorify a folly so, to wish thee to advance,

rhyme with the line which follows it, entirely changes and spoils the movement of the passage.

οὔτε κεν αὐτὸς ἐνὶ πρώτοισι μαχοίμην,
οὔτε κέ σε στέλλοιμι μάχην ἐς κυδιάνειραν.[1]

Neither would I myself go forth to fight with the foremost,
Nor would I urge thee on to enter the glorious battle,

says Homer; there he stops, and begins an opposed movement:

νῦν δ᾽—ἔμπης γὰρ Κῆρες ἐφεστᾶσιν θανάτοιο—

But—for a thousand fates of death stand close to us always—

This line, in which Homer wishes to go away with the most
marked rapidity from the line before, Chapman is forced, by
the necessity of rhyming, intimately to connect with the line
before.

But since we *must* go, though not here, and that, besides the chance.

The moment the word *chance* strikes our ear, we are irresistibly
carried back to *advance* and to the whole previous line, which,
according to Homer's own feeling, we ought to have left
behind us entirely, and to be moving farther and farther away
from.

Rhyme certainly, by intensifying antithesis, can intensify
separation, and this is precisely what Pope does; but this balanced
rhetorical antithesis, though very effective, is entirely un-
Homeric. And this is what I mean by saying that Pope fails to
render Homer, because he does not render his plainness and
directness of style and diction. Where Homer marks separation
by moving away, Pope marks it by antithesis. No passage could
show this better than the passage I have just quoted. . . .

A literary and intellectualized language is, however, in its
own way well suited to grand matters; and Pope, with a
language of this kind and his own admirable talent, comes off
well enough as long as he has passion, or oratory, or a great
crisis to deal with. Even here, as I have been pointing out, he
does not render Homer; but he and his style are in themselves

[1] *Iliad*, xii. 324.

strong. It is when he comes to level passages, passages of narrative or description, that he and his style are sorely tried, and prove themselves weak. A perfectly plain direct style can of course convey the simplest matter as naturally as the grandest; indeed, it must be harder for it, one would say, to convey a grand matter worthily and nobly, than to convey a common matter as, alone such a matter should be conveyed, plainly and simply. But the style of Rasselas is incomparably better fitted to describe a sage philosophising than a soldier lighting his campfire. The style of Pope is not the style of Rasselas; but it is equally a literary style, equally unfitted to describe a simple matter with the plain naturalness of Homer.

Everyone knows the passage at the end of the eighth book of the *Iliad*, where the fires of the Trojan encampment are likened to the stars. It is very far from my wish to hold Pope up to ridicule, so I shall not quote the commencement of the passage, which in the original is of great and celebrated beauty, and in translating which Pope has been singularly and notoriously fortunate. But the latter part of the passage, where Homer leaves the stars, and comes to the Trojan fires, treats of the plainest, most matter-of-fact subject possible, and deals with this, as Homer always deals with every subject, in the plainest and most straightforward style. 'So many in number, between the ships and the streams of Xanthus, shone forth in front of Troy the fires kindled by the Trojans. There were kindled a thousand fires in the plain; and by each one there sat fifty men in the light of the blazing fire. And the horses, munching white barley and rye, and standing by the chariots, waited for the bright-throned Morning.'[1]

In Pope's translation, this plain story becomes the following:

> So many flames before proud Ilion blaze,
> And brighten glimmering Xanthus with their rays;
> The long reflections of the distant fires
> Gleam on the walls, and tremble on the spires.

[1] *Iliad*, viii. 560.

A thousand piles the dusky horrors gild,
And shoot a shady lustre o'er the field.
Full fifty guards each flaming pile attend,
Whose umbered arms, by fits, thick flashes send;
Loud neigh the coursers o'er their heaps of corn,
And ardent warriors wait the rising morn.

It is for passages of this sort, which, after all, form the bulk of a narrative poem, that Pope's style is so bad. In elevated passages he is powerful, as Homer is powerful, though not in the same way; but in plain narrative, where Homer is still powerful and delightful, Pope, by the inherent fault of his style, is ineffective and out of taste. Wordsworth says somewhere, that wherever Virgil seems to have composed 'with his eye on the object', Dryden fails to render him. Homer invariably composes 'with his eye on the object', whether the object be a moral or a material one: Pope composes with his eye on his style, into which he translates his object, whatever it is. That, therefore, which Homer conveys to us immediately, Pope conveys to us through a medium. He aims at turning Homer's sentiments pointedly and rhetorically; at investing Homer's description with ornament and dignity. A sentiment may be changed by being put into a pointed and oratorical form, yet may still be very effective in that form; but a description, the moment it takes its eyes off that which it is to describe, and begins to think of ornamenting itself, is worthless.

Therefore, I say, the translator of Homer should penetrate himself with a sense of the plainness and directness of Homer's style; of the simplicity with which Homer's thought is evolved and expressed. He has Pope's fate before his eyes, to show him what a divorce may be created even between the most gifted translator and Homer by an artificial evolution of thought and a literary cast of style.

from *Essays in Criticism*, First Series

The Study of Poetry

. . . There can be no more useful help for discovering what poetry belongs to the class of the truly excellent, and can there-fore do us most good, than to have always in one's mind lines and expressions of the great masters, and to apply them as a touchstone to other poetry. Of course we are not to require this other poetry to resemble them; it may be very dissimilar. But if we have any tact we shall find them, when we have lodged them well in our minds, an infallible touchstone for detecting the presence or absence of high poetic quality, and also the degree of this quality, in all other poetry which we may place beside them. Short passages, even single lines, will serve our turn quite sufficiently. Take the two lines which I have just quoted from Homer, the poet's comment on Helen's mention of her brothers;—or take his

ᵉΑ δειλώ, τί σφῶϊ δόμεν Πηλῆϊ ἄνακτι
Θνητῷ; ὑμεῖς δ' ἐστὸν ἀγήρω τ' ἀθανάτω τε.
ἢ ἵνα δυστήνοισι μετ' ἀνδράσιν ἄλγε' ἔχητον;[1]

the address of Zeus to the horses of Peleus;—or take finally this

Καὶ σέ, γέρον, τὸ πρὶν μὲν ἀκούομεν ὄλβιον εἶναι.[2]

[1] 'Ah, unhappy pair, why gave we you to King Peleus, to a mortal? but ye are without old age, and immortal. Was it that with men born in misery ye might have sorrow?'—*Iliad*, xvii. 443-445.

[2] 'Nay, and thou too, old man, in former days wast, as we hear, happy.'—*Iliad*, xxiv. 543.

the words of Achilles to Priam, a suppliant before him. Take that incomparable line and a half of Dante, Ugolino's tremendous words:—

> Io no piangeva; sì dentro impietrai.
> Piangevan elli . . .[1]

take the lovely words of Beatrice to Virgil—

> Io son fatta da Dio, sua mercè, tale,
> Che la vostra miseria non mi tange,
> Nè fiamma d' esto incendio non m' assale . . .[2]

take the simple, but perfect, single line—

> In la sua volontade è nostra pace.[3]

Take of Shakespeare a line or two of Henry the Fourth's expostulation with sleep—

> Wilt thou upon the high and giddy mast
> Seal up the ship-boy's eyes, and rock his brains
> In cradle of the rude imperious surge . . .

and take, as well, Hamlet's dying request to Horatio—

> If thou didst ever hold me in thy heart,
> Absent thee from felicity awhile,
> And in this harsh world draw thy breath in pain
> To tell my story . . .

Take of Milton that Miltonic passage—

>   Darken'd so, yet shone
> Above them all the archangel; but his face
> Deep scars of thunder had intrench'd, and care
> Sat on his faded cheek . . .

[1] 'I wailed not, so of stone grew I within;—*they* wailed.'—*Inferno*, xxxiii. 39, 40.

[2] 'Of such sort hath God, thanked be His mercy, made me, that your misery toucheth me not, neither doth the flame of this fire strike me.' —*Inferno*, ii. 91–93.

[3] 'In His will is our peace.'—*Paradiso*, iii. 85.

add two such lines as—

> And courage never to submit or yield
> And what is else not to be overcome . . .

and finish with the exquisite close to the loss of Proserpine, the loss

> . . . which cost Ceres all that pain
> To seek her through the world.

These few lines, if we have tact and can use them, are enough even of themselves to keep clear and sound our judgments about poetry, to save us from fallacious estimates of it, to conduct us to a real estimate.

The specimens I have quoted differ widely from one another, but they have in common this: the possession of the very highest poetical quality. If we are thoroughly penetrated by their power, we shall find that we have acquired a sense enabling us, whatever poetry may be laid before us, to feel the degree in which a high poetical quality is present or wanting there. Critics give themselves great labour to draw out what in the abstract constitutes the characters of a high quality of poetry. It is much better simply to have recourse to concrete examples; —to take specimens of poetry of the high, the very highest, quality, and to say: The characters of a high quality of poetry are what is expressed *there*. They are far better recognized by being felt in the verse of the master, than by being perused in the prose of the critic. Nevertheless if we are urgently pressed to give some critical account of them, we may safely, perhaps, venture on laying down, not indeed how and why the characters arise, but where and in what they arise. They are in the matter and substance of the poetry, and they are in its manner and style. Both of these, the substance and matter on the one hand, the style and manner on the other, have a mark, an accent, of high beauty, worth, and power. But if we are asked to define this mark and accent in the abstract, our answer must be: No, for we should thereby be darkening the question, not clearing it.

The mark and accent are as given by the substance and matter of that poetry, by the style and manner of that poetry, and of all other poetry which is akin to it in quality.

Only one thing we may add as to the substance and matter of poetry, guiding ourselves by Aristotle's profound observation that the superiority of poetry over history consists in its possessing a higher truth and a higher seriousness (φιλοσοφώτερον καὶ σπουδαιότερον). Let us add, therefore, to what we have said, this: that the substance and matter of the best poetry acquire their special character from possessing, in an eminent degree, truth and seriousness. We may add yet further what is in itself evident, that to the style and manner of the best poetry their special character, their accent, is given by their diction, and, even yet more, by their movement. And though we distinguish between the two characters, the two accents, of superiority, yet they are nevertheless vitally connected one with the other. The superior character of truth and seriousness, in the matter and substance of the best poetry, is inseparable from the superiority of diction and movement marking its style and manner. The two superiorities are closely related, and are in steadfast proportion one to the other. So far as high poetic truth and seriousness are wanting to a poet's matter and substance, so far also, we may be sure, will a high poetic stamp of diction and movement be wanting to his style and manner. In proportion as this high stamp of diction and movement, again, is absent from a poet's style and manner, we shall find, also, that high poetic truth and seriousness are absent from his substance and matter.

from *Essays in Criticism*, Second Series

Poetry and Life

... To exhibit [the] body of Wordsworth's best work, to clear away obstructions from around it, and to let it speak for itself, is what every lover of Wordsworth should desire. Until this has been done, Wordsworth, whom we, to whom he is dear, all of us know and feel to be so great a poet, has not had a fair chance before the world. When once it has been done, he will make his way best, not by our advocacy of him, but by his own worth and power. We may safely leave him to make his way thus, we who believe that a superior worth and power in poetry finds in mankind a sense responsive to it and disposed at last to recognize it. Yet at the outset, before he has been duly known and recognized, we may do Wordsworth a service, perhaps by indicating in what his superior power and worth will be found to consist, and in what it will not.

Long ago, in speaking of Homer, I said that the noble and profound application of ideas to life is the most essential part of poetic greatness. I said that a great poet receives his distinctive character of superiority from his application, under the conditions immutably fixed by the laws of poetic beauty and poetic truth, from his application, I say, to his subject, whatever it may be, of the ideas

On man, on nature, and on human life,

which he has acquired for himself. The line quoted is Wordsworth's own; and his superiority arises from his powerful use, in his best pieces, his powerful application to his subject, of ideas 'on man, on nature, and on human life'.

Voltaire, with his signal acuteness, most truly remarked that 'no nation has treated in poetry moral ideas with more energy and depth than the English nation'. And he adds: 'There, it seems to me, is the great merit of the English poets.' Voltaire does not mean, by 'treating in poetry moral ideas', the composing moral and didactic poems;—that brings us but a very little way in poetry. He means just the same thing as was meant when I spoke above 'of the noble and profound application of ideas to life'; and he means the application of these ideas under the conditions fixed for us by the laws of poetic beauty and poetic truth. If it is said that to call these ideas *moral* ideas is to introduce a strong and injurious limitation, I answer that it is to do nothing of the kind, because moral ideas are really so main a part of human life. The question, *how to live*, is itself a moral idea; and it is the question which most interests every man, and with which, in some way or other, he is perpetually occupied. A large sense is of course to be given to the term *moral*. Whatever bears upon the question, 'how to live', comes under it.

> Nor love thy life, nor hate; but, what thou liv'st,
> Live well; how long or short, permit to heaven.

In those fine lines Milton utters, as every one at once perceives, a moral idea. Yes, but so too, when Keats consoles the forward-bending lover on the Grecian Urn, the lover arrested and presented in immortal relief by the sculptor's hand before he can kiss, with the line,

> For ever wilt thou love, and she be fair—

he utters a moral idea. When Shakespeare says that

> We are such stuff
> As dreams are made on, and our little life
> Is rounded with a sleep,

he utters a moral idea.

Voltaire was right in thinking that the energetic and profound treatment of moral ideas, in this large sense, is what distinguishes the English poetry. He sincerely meant praise, not dispraise or hint of limitation; and they err who suppose that poetic limitation is a necessary consequence of the fact, the fact being granted as Voltaire states it. If what distinguishes the greatest poets is their powerful and profound application of ideas to life, which surely no good critic will deny, then to prefix to the term ideas here the term moral makes hardly any difference, because human life itself is in so preponderating a degree moral.

It is important, therefore, to hold fast to this: that poetry is at bottom a criticism of life; that the greatness of a poet lies in his powerful and beautiful application of ideas to life,—to the question: How to live? Morals are often treated in a narrow and false fashion; they are bound up with systems of thought and belief which have had their day; they are fallen into the hands of pedants and professional dealers; they grow tiresome to some of us. We find attraction, at times, even in a poetry of revolt against them; in a poetry which might take for its motto Omar Khayam's words: 'Let us make up in the tavern for the time which we have wasted in the mosque.' Or we find attractions in a poetry indifferent to them; in a poetry where the contents may be what they will, but where the form is studied and exquisite. We delude ourselves in either case; and the best cure for our delusion is to let our minds rest upon that great and inexhaustible word *life*, until we learn to enter into its meaning. A poetry of revolt against moral ideas is a poetry of revolt against *life*; a poetry of indifference towards moral ideas is a poetry of indifference towards *life*.

Epictetus had a happy figure for things like the play of the senses, or literary form and finish, or argumentative ingenuity, in comparison with 'the best and master thing', for us, as he called it, the concern, how to live. Some people were afraid of them, he said, or they disliked and undervalued them. Such people were wrong; they were unthankful or cowardly. But the things might also be over-prized, and treated as final when they are not. They bear to life the relation which inns bear to home. 'As if a man, journeying home, and finding a nice inn on the road, and liking it, were to stay for ever at the inn! Man, thou hast forgotten thine object; thy journey was not *to* this, but *through* this. "But this inn is taking." And how many other inns, too, are taking, and how many fields and meadows! but as places of passage merely. You have an object, which is this: to get home, to do your duty to your family, friends, and fellow-countrymen, to attain inward freedom, serenity, happiness, contentment. Style takes your fancy, arguing takes your fancy, and you forget your home and want to make your abode with them and to stay with them, on the plea that they are taking. Who denies that they are taking? but as places of passage, as inns. And when I say this, you suppose me to be attacking the care for style, the care for argument. I am not; I attack the resting in them, the not looking to the end which is beyond them.'

Now, when we come across a poet like Théophile Gautier, we have a poet who has taken up his abode at an inn, and never got farther. There may be inducements to this or that one of us, at this or that moment, to find delight in him, to cleave to him; but after all, we do not change the truth about him,—we only stay ourselves in his inn along with him. And when we come across a poet like Wordsworth, who sings

> Of truth, of grandeur, beauty, love and hope.
> And melancholy fear subdued by faith,
> Of blessed consolations in distress,
> Of moral strength and intellectual power,
> Of joy in widest commonalty spread—

then we have a poet intent on 'the best and master thing', and who prosecutes his journey home. We say, for brevity's sake, that he deals with *life*, because he deals with that in which life really consists. This is what Voltaire means to praise in the English poets,—this dealing with what is really life. But always it is the mark of the greatest poets that they deal with it; and to say that the English poets are remarkable for dealing with it, is only another way of saying what is true, that in poetry the English genius has especially shown its power.

Wordsworth deals with it, and his greatness lies in his dealing with it so powerfully. I have named a number of celebrated poets above all of whom he, in my opinion, deserves to be placed. He is to be placed above poets like Voltaire, Dryden, Pope, Lessing, Schiller, because these famous personages, with a thousand gifts and merits, never, or scarcely ever, attain the distinctive accent and utterance of the high and genuine poets—

Quique pii vates et Phoebo digna locuti,[1]

at all. Burns, Keats, Heine, not to speak of others in our list, have this accent;—who can doubt it? And at the same time they have treasures of humour, felicity, passion, for which in Wordsworth we shall look in vain. Where, then, is Wordsworth's superiority? It is here; he deals with more of *life* than they do; he deals with *life*, as a whole, more powerfully.

No Wordsworthian will doubt this. Nay, the fervent Wordsworthian will add, as Mr. Leslie Stephen does, that Wordsworth's poetry is precious because his philosophy is sound; that his 'ethical system is as distinctive and capable of exposition as Bishop Butler's'; that his poetry is informed by ideas which 'fall spontaneously into a scientific system of thought'. But we must be on our guard against the Wordsworthians if we want to secure for Wordsworth his due rank as a poet. The Wordsworthians are apt to praise him for the wrong things, and to lay far too much stress upon what they call his philosophy. His poetry is the reality, his philosophy,— so far, at least, as it may put on the form and habit of 'a scientific system of thought', and the more that it puts them on,—is the illusion. Perhaps we shall one day learn to make this proposition general, and to say: Poetry is the reality, philosophy, the illusion. But in Wordsworth's case, at any rate, we cannot do him justice until we dismiss his formal philosophy.

from 'Wordsworth' in *Essays in Criticism*, Second Series

---

[1] 'Poets with a sense of duty who spoke things worthy of Phoebus [god of music and poetry].'

Sweetness and Light

. . . But there is of culture another view, in which not solely the scientific passion, the sheer desire to see things as they are, natural and proper in an intelligent being, appears as the ground of it. There is a view in which all the love of our neighbour, the impulses towards action, help, and beneficence, the desire for removing human error, clearing human confusion, and diminishing human misery, the noble aspiration to leave the world better and happier than we found it,—motives eminently such as are called social,—come in as part of the grounds of culture, and the main and pre-eminent part. Culture is then properly described not as having its origin in curiosity, but as having its origin in the love of perfection; it is *a study of perfection*. It moves by the force, not merely or primarily of the scientific passion for pure knowledge, but also of the moral and social passion for doing good. As, in the first view of it, we took for its worthy motto Montesquieu's words: 'To render an intelligent being yet more intelligent!' so, in the second view of it, there is no better motto which it can have than these words of Bishop Wilson: 'To make reason and the will of God prevail!'

Only, whereas the passion for doing good is apt to be over-hasty in determining what reason and the will of God say, because its turn is for acting rather than thinking and it wants to be beginning to act; and whereas it is apt to take its own conceptions, which proceed from its own state of development and share in all the imperfections and immaturities of this, for a basis of action; what distinguishes culture is, that it is possessed by the scientific passion as well as by the passion of doing good; that it demands worthy notions of reason and the will of God, and does not readily suffer its own crude conceptions to substitute themselves for them. And knowing that no action or institution can be salutary and stable which is not based on reason and the will of God, it is not so bent on acting and instituting, even with the great aim of diminishing human error and misery ever before its thoughts, but that it can remember that acting and instituting are of little use, unless we know how and what we ought to act and to institute.

This culture is more interesting and more far-reaching than that other, which is founded solely on the scientific passion for knowing. But it needs times of faith and ardour, times when the intellectual horizon is opening and widening all round us, to flourish in. And is not the close and bounded intellectual horizon within which we have long lived and moved now lifting up, and are not new lights finding free passage to shine in upon us? For a long time there was no passage for them to make their way in upon us, and then it was of no use to think of adapting the world's action to them. Where was the hope of making reason and the will of God prevail among people who had a routine which they had christened reason and the will of God, in which they were inextricably bound, and beyond which they had no power of looking? But now the iron force of adhesion to the old routine,—social, political, religious,—has wonderfully yielded; the iron force of exclusion of all which is new has wonderfully yielded. The danger now is, not that people should obstinately refuse to allow anything but their old routine to pass for reason and the will of God, but either that they should allow some novelty or other to pass for these too easily, or else that they should underrate the importance of them altogether, and think it enough to follow action for its own sake, without troubling themselves to make reason and the will of God prevail therein. Now, then, is the moment for culture to be of service, culture which believes in making reason and the will of God prevail, believes in perfection, is the study and pursuit of perfection, and is no longer debarred, by a rigid invincible exclusion of whatever is new, from getting acceptance for its ideas, simply because they are new.

The moment this view of culture is seized, the moment it is regarded not solely as the endeavour to see things as they are, to draw towards a knowledge of the universal order which seems to be intended and aimed at in the world, and which it is a man's happiness to go along with or his misery to go counter to,—to learn, in short, the will of God,—the moment, I say, culture is considered not merely as the endeavour to *see* and *learn* this, but as the endeavour, also, to make it *prevail*, the moral, social, and beneficent character of culture becomes manifest. The mere endeavour to see and learn the truth for our own personal satisfaction is indeed a commencement for making it prevail, a preparing the way for this, which always serves this, and is wrongly, therefore, stamped with blame absolutely in itself and not only in its caricature and degeneration. But perhaps it has got stamped with blame, and disparaged with the dubious title of curiosity, because in comparison with this wider endeavour of such great and plain utility it looks selfish, petty, and unprofitable.

And religion, the greatest and most important of the efforts by which the human race has manifested its impulse to perfect itself,—religion, that voice of the deepest human experience,—does not only enjoin and sanction the aim which is the great aim of culture, the aim of setting ourselves to ascertain what perfection is and to make it prevail; but also, in determining generally in what human perfection consists, religion comes to a conclusion identical with that which culture,—culture seeking the determination of this question through *all* the voices of human experience which have been heard upon it, of art, science, poetry, philosophy, history, as well as of religion, in order to give a greater fulness and certainty to its solution,— likewise reaches. Religion says: *The kingdom of God is within you;* and culture, in like manner, places human perfection in an *internal* condition, in the growth and predominance of our humanity proper, as distinguished from our animality. It places it in the ever-increasing efficacy and in the general harmonious expansion of those gifts of thought and feeling, which make the peculiar dignity, wealth, and happiness of human nature. As I have said on a former occasion: 'It is in making endless additions to itself, in the endless expansion of its powers, in endless growth in wisdom and beauty, that the spirit of the human race finds its ideal. To reach this ideal, culture is an indispensable aid, and that is the true value of culture.' Not a having and a resting, but a growing and a becoming, is the character of perfection as culture conceives it; and here, too, it coincides with religion.

And because men are all members of one great whole, and the sympathy which is in human nature will not allow one member to be indifferent to the rest or to have a perfect welfare independent of the rest, the expansion of our humanity, to suit the idea of perfection which culture forms, must be a *general* expansion. Perfection, as culture conceives it, is not possible while the individual remains isolated. The individual is required, under pain of being stunted and enfeebled in his own development if he disobeys, to carry others along with him in his march towards perfection, to be continually doing all he can to enlarge and increase the volume of the human stream sweeping thitherward. And here, once more, culture lays on us the same obligation as religion which says, as Bishop Wilson has admirably put it, that 'to promote the kingdom of God is to increase and hasten one's own happiness'.

But, finally, perfection,—as culture from a thorough disinterested study of human nature and human experience learns to conceive it,—is a harmonious expansion of *all* the powers which make the beauty and worth of human nature, and is not consistent with the over-development of any one power at the expense of the rest. Here culture goes beyond religion, as religion is generally conceived by us.

If culture, then, is a study of perfection, and of harmonious perfection, general perfection, and perfection which consists in becoming something rather than in having something, in an inward condition of the mind and spirit, not in an outward set of circumstances,—it is clear that culture, instead of being the frivolous and useless thing which Mr. Bright, and Mr. Frederic Harrison, and many other Liberals are apt to call it, has a very important function to fulfil for mankind. And this function is particularly important in our modern world, of which the whole civilization is, to a much greater degree than the civilization of Greece and Rome, mechanical and external, and tends constantly to become more so. But above all in our own country has culture a weighty part to perform, because here that mechanical character, which civilization tends to take everywhere, is shown in the most eminent degree. Indeed nearly all the characters of perfection, as culture teaches us to fix them, meet in this country with some powerful tendency which thwarts them and sets them at defiance. The idea of perfection as an *inward* condition of the mind and spirit is at variance with the mechanical and material civilization in esteem with us, and nowhere, as I have said, so much in esteem as with us. The idea of perfection as a *general* expansion of the human family is at variance with our strong individualism, our hatred of all limits to the unrestrained swing of the individual's personality, our maxim of 'every man for himself'. Above all, the idea of perfection as a *harmonious* expansion of human nature is at variance with our want of flexibility, with our inaptitude for seeing more than one side of a thing, with our intense energetic absorption in the particular pursuit we happen to be following. So culture has a rough task to achieve in this country. Its preachers have, and are likely long to have, a hard time of it, and they will much oftener be regarded, for a great while to come, as elegant or spurious Jeremiahs than as friends and benefactors. That, however, will not prevent their doing in the end good service if they persevere. And, meanwhile, the mode of action they have to pursue, and the sort of habits they must fight against, ought to be made quite clear for every one to see, who may be willing to look at the matter attentively and dispassionately.

Faith in machinery, is, I said, our besetting danger; often in machinery most absurdly disproportioned to the end which this machinery, if it is to do any good at all, is to serve; but always in machinery, as if it had a value in and for itself. What is freedom but machinery? what is population but machinery? what is coal but machinery? what are railroads but machinery? what is wealth but machinery? what are, even, religious organizations but machinery? Now almost every voice in England is accustomed to speak of these things as if they were precious ends in themselves, and therefore had some of the characters of perfection indisputably joined to them. I have before now noticed Mr. Roebuck's stock argument for proving the greatness and happiness of England as she is, and for quite stopping the mouths of all gainsayers. Mr. Roebuck is never weary of reiterating this argument of his, so I do not know why I should be weary of noticing it. 'May not every man in England say what he likes?'—Mr. Roebuck perpetually asks; and that, he thinks, is quite sufficient, and when every man may say what he likes, our aspirations ought to be satisfied. But the aspirations of culture, which is the study of perfection, are not satisfied, unless what men say, when they may say what they like, is worth saying,—has good in it, and more good than bad. In the same way the *Times*, replying to some foreign strictures on the dress, looks, and behaviour of the English abroad, urges that the English ideal is that every one should be free to do and to look just as he likes. But culture indefatigably tries, not to make what each raw person may like the rule by which he fashions himself; but to draw ever nearer to a sense of what is indeed beautiful, graceful, and becoming, and to get the raw person to like that.

And in the same way with respect to railroads and coal. Every one must have observed the strange language current during the late discussions as to the possible failures of our supplies of coal. Our coal, thousands of people were saying, is the real basis of our national greatness; if our coal runs short, there is an end of the greatness of England. But what *is* greatness?— culture makes us ask. Greatness is a spiritual condition worthy to excite love, interest, and admiration; and the outward proof of possessing greatness is that we excite love, interest, and admiration. If England were swallowed up by the sea to-morrow, which of the two, a hundred years hence, would most excite the love, interest, and admiration of mankind,—would most, therefore, show the evidences of having possessed greatness,— the England of the last twenty years, or the England of Elizabeth, of a time of splendid spiritual effort, but when our coal, and our industrial operations depending on coal, were very little developed? Well, then, what an unsound habit of mind it must be which makes us talk of things like coal or iron as constituting the greatness of England, and how salutary a friend is culture, bent on seeing things as they are, and thus dissipating delusions of this kind and fixing standards of perfection that are real!

Wealth, again, that end to which our prodigious works for material advantage are directed,—the commonest of common-places tells us how men are always apt to regard wealth as a precious end in itself; and certainly they have never been so apt thus to regard it as they are in England at the present time. Never did people believe anything more firmly than nine Englishmen out of ten at the present day believe that our greatness and welfare are proved by our being so very rich. Now, the use of culture is that it helps us, by means of its spiritual standard of perfection, to regard wealth as but machinery, and not only to say as a matter of words that we regard wealth as but machinery, but really to perceive and feel that it is so. If it were not for this purging effect wrought upon our minds by culture, the whole world, the future as well as the present, would inevitably belong to the Philistines. The people who believe most that our greatness and welfare are proved by our being very rich, and who most give their lives and thoughts to be-coming rich, are just the very people whom we call Philistines. Culture says: 'Consider these people, then, their way of life, their habits, their manners, the very tones of their voice; look at them attentively; observe the literature they read, the things which give them pleasure, the words which come forth out of their mouths, the thoughts which make the furniture of their minds; would any amount of wealth be worth having with the condition that one was to become just like these people by having it?' And thus culture begets a dissatisfaction which is of the highest possible value in stemming the common tide of men's thoughts in a wealthy and industrial community, and which saves the future, as one may hope, from being vulgarized, even if it cannot save the present.

Population, again, and bodily health and vigour, are things which are nowhere treated in such an unintelligent, misleading, exaggerated way as in England. Both are really machinery; yet how many people all around us do we see rest in them and fail to look beyond them! Why, one has heard people, fresh from reading certain articles of the *Times* on the Registrar-General's returns of marriages and births in this country, who would talk of our large English families in quite a solemn strain, as if they had something in itself beautiful, elevating, and meritorious in them; as if the British Philistine would have only to present himself before the Great Judge with his twelve children, in order to be received among the sheep as a matter of right!

But bodily health and vigour, it may be said, are not to be classed with wealth and population as mere machinery; they have a more real and essential value. True; but only as they are more intimately connected with a perfect spiritual condition than wealth or population are. The moment we disjoin them from the idea of a perfect spiritual condition, and pursue them, as we do pursue them, for their own sake and as ends in themselves, our worship of them becomes as mere worship of machinery, as our worship of wealth or population, and as unintelligent and vulgarizing a worship as that is. Every one with anything like an adequate idea of human perfection has distinctly marked this subordination to higher and spiritual ends of the cultivation of bodily vigour and activity. 'Bodily exercise profiteth little; but godliness is profitable unto all things,' says the author of the Epistle to Timothy. And the utilitarian Franklin says just as explicitly:—'Eat and drink such an exact quantity as suits the constitution of thy body, *in reference to the services of the mind.*' But the point of view of culture, keeping the mark of human perfection simply and broadly in view, and not assigning to this perfection, as religion or utilitarianism assigns to it, a special and limited character, this point of view, I say, of culture is best given by these words of Epictetus:—'It is a sigh of ἀφυΐα,' says he,—that is, of a nature not finely tempered,— 'to give yourselves up to things which relate to the body; to make, for instance, a great fuss about exercise, a great fuss about eating, a great fuss about drinking, a great fuss about walking, a great fuss about riding. All these things ought to be done merely by the way: the formation of the spirit and character must be our real concern.' This is admirable; and, indeed, the Greek word εὐφυΐα, a finely tempered nature, gives exactly the notion of perfection as culture brings us to conceive it: a harmonious perfection, a perfection in which the characters of beauty and intelligence are both present, which unites 'the two noblest of things',—as Swift, who of one of the two, at any rate, had himself all too little, most happily calls them in his *Battle of the Books,*—'the two noblest of things, *sweetness and light*'. The εὐφυής is the man who tends towards sweetness and light; the ἀφυής, on the other hand, is our Philistine. The immense spiritual significance of the Greeks is due to their having been inspired with this central and happy idea of the essential character of human perfection; and Mr. Bright's misconception of culture, as a smattering of Greek and Latin, comes itself, after all, from this wonderful significance of the Greeks having affected the very machinery of our education, and is in itself a kind of homage to it.

In thus making sweetness and light to be characters of perfection, culture is of like spirit with poetry, follows one law with poetry. Far more than on our freedom, our population, and our industrialism, many amongst us rely upon our religious organizations to save us. I have called religion a yet more important manifestation of human nature than poetry, because it has worked on a broader scale for perfection, and with greater masses of men. But the idea of beauty and of a human nature perfect on all its sides, which is the dominant idea of poetry, is a true and invaluable idea, though it has not yet had the success that the idea of conquering the obvious faults of our animality, and of a human nature perfect on the moral side,—which is the dominant idea of religion,—has been enabled to have; and it is destined, adding to itself the religious idea of a devout energy, to transform and govern the other. . . .

Nothing is more common than for people to confound the inward peace and satisfaction which follows the subduing of the obvious faults of our animality with what I may call absolute inward peace and satisfaction,—the peace and satisfaction which are reached as we draw near to complete spiritual perfection, and not merely to moral perfection, or rather to relative moral perfection. No people in the world have done more and struggled more to attain this relative moral perfection than our English race has. For no people in the world has the command to *resist the devil*, to *overcome the wicked one*, in the nearest and most obvious sense of these words, had such a pressing force and reality. And we have had our reward, not only in the great worldly prosperity which our obedience to this command has brought us, but also, and far more, in great inward peace and satisfaction. But to me few things are more pathetic than to see people, on the strength of the inward peace and satisfaction which their rudimentary efforts towards perfection have brought them, employ, concerning their incomplete perfection and the religious organizations within which they have found it, language which properly applies only to complete perfection, and is a far-off echo of the human soul's prophecy of it. Religion itself, I need hardly say, supplies them in abundance with this grand language. And very freely do they use it; yet it is really the severest possible criticism of such an incomplete perfection as alone we have yet reached through our religious organizations.

The impulse of the English race towards moral development and self-conquest has nowhere so powerfully manifested itself as in Puritanism. Nowhere has Puritanism found so adequate an expression as in the religious organization of the Independents. The modern Independents have a newspaper, the *Nonconformist*, written with great sincerity and ability. The motto, the standard, the profession of faith which this organ of theirs carries aloft, is: 'The Dissidence of Dissent and the Protestantism of the Protestant religion.' There is sweetness and light, and an ideal of complete harmonious human perfection! One need not go to culture and poetry to find language to judge it. Religion, with its instinct for perfection, supplies language to judge it, language, too, which is in our mouths every day. 'Finally, be of one mind, united in feeling,' says St. Peter. There is an ideal which judges the Puritan ideal: 'The Dissidence of Dissent and the Protestantism of the Protestant religion!' And religious organizations like this are what people believe in, rest in, would give their lives for! Such, I say, is the wonderful virtue of even the beginnings of perfection, of having conquered even the plain faults of our animality, that the religious organization which has helped us to do it can seem to us something precious, salutary, and to be propagated, even when it wears such a brand of imperfection on its forehead as this. And men have got such a habit of giving to the language of religion a special application, of making it a mere jargon, that for the condemnation which religion itself passes on the shortcomings of their religious organizations they have no ear; they are sure to cheat themselves and to explain this condemnation away. They can only be reached by the criticism which culture, like poetry, speaking a language not to be sophisticated, and resolutely testing these organizations by the ideal of a human perfection complete on all sides, applies to them.

But men of culture and poetry, it will be said, are again and again failing, and failing conspicuously, in the necessary first stage to a harmonious perfection, in the subduing of the great obvious faults of our animality, which it is the glory of these religious organizations to have helped us to subdue. True, they do often so fail. They have often been without the virtues as well as the faults of the Puritan; it has been one of their dangers that they so felt the Puritan's faults that they too much neglected the practice of his virtues. I will not, however, exculpate them at the Puritan's expense. They have often failed in morality, and morality is indispensable. And they have been punished for their failure, as the Puritan has been rewarded for his performance. They have been punished wherein they erred; but their ideal of beauty, of sweetness and light, and a human nature complete on all its sides, remains the true ideal of perfection still; just as the Puritan's ideal of perfection remains narrow and inadequate, although for what he did well he has been richly rewarded. Notwithstanding the mighty results of the Pilgrim Fathers' voyage, they and their standard of perfection are rightly judged when we figure to ourselves Shakespeare or Virgil,—souls in whom sweetness and light, and all that in human nature is most humane, were eminent,—accompanying them on their voyage, and think what intolerable company Shakespeare and Virgil would have found them! In the same way let us judge the religious organizations which we see all around us. Do not let us deny the good and the happiness which they have accomplished; but do not let us fail to see clearly that their idea of human perfection is narrow and inadequate, and that the Dissidence of Dissent and the Protestantism of the Protestant religion will never bring humanity to its true goal. As I said with regard to wealth: Let us look at the life of those who live in and for it,—so I say with regard to the religious organizations. Look at the life imaged in such a newspaper as the *Nonconformist*,—a life of jealousy of the Establishment, disputes, tea-meetings, openings of chapels, sermons; and then think of it as an ideal of a human life completing itself on all sides, and aspiring with all its organs after sweetness, light, and perfection!

Another newspaper, representing, like the *Nonconformist*, one of the religious organizations of this country, was a short time ago giving an account of the crowd at Epsom on the Derby day, and of all the vice and hideousness which was to be seen in that crowd; and then the writer turned suddenly round upon Professor Huxley, and asked him how he proposed to cure all this vice and hideousness without religion. I confess I felt disposed to ask the asker this question: and how do you propose to cure it with such a religion as yours? How is the ideal of a life so unlovely, so unattractive, so incomplete, so narrow, so far removed from a true and satisfying ideal of human perfection, as is the life of your religious organization as you yourself reflect it, to conquer and transform all this vice and hideousness? Indeed, the strongest plea for the study of perfection as pursued by culture, the clearest proof of the actual inadequacy of the idea of perfection held by the religious organizations,—expressing, as I have said, the most widespread effort which the human race has yet made after perfection,—is to be found in the state of our life and society with these in possession of it, and having been in possession of it I know not how many hundred years. We are all of us included in some religious organization or other; we all call ourselves, in the sublime and aspiring language of religion which I have before noticed, *children of God.* Children of God;—it is an immense pretension!—and how are we to justify it? By the works which we do, and the words which we speak. And the work which we collective children of God do, our grand centre of life, our *city* which we have builded for us to dwell in, is London! London, with its unutterable external hideousness, and with its internal canker of *publicè egestas, privatim opulentia,*—to use the words which Sallust puts into Cato's mouth about Rome,—unequalled in the world! The word, again, which we children of God speak, the voice which most hits our collective thought, the newspaper with the largest circulation in England, nay, with the largest circulation in the whole world, is the *Daily Telegraph!* I say that when our religious organizations,—which I admit to express the most considerable effort after perfection that our race has yet made,—land us in no better result than this, it is high time to examine carefully their idea of perfection, to see whether it does not leave out of account sides and forces of human nature which we might turn to great use; whether it would not be more operative if it were more complete. And I say that the English reliance on our religious organizations and on their ideas of human perfection just as they stand, is like our reliance on freedom, on muscular Christianity, on population, on coal, on wealth,—mere belief in machinery, and unfruitful; and that it is wholesomely counteracted by culture, bent on seeing things as they are, and on drawing the human race onwards to a more complete, a harmonious perfection.

Culture, however, shows its single-minded love of perfection, its desire simply to make reason and the will of God prevail, its freedom from fanaticism, by its attitude towards all this machinery, even while it insists that it *is* machinery. Fanatics, seeing the mischief men do themselves by their blind belief in some machinery or other,—whether it is wealth and industrialism, or whether it is the cultivation of bodily strength and activity, or whether it is a political organization,—or whether it is a religious organization,—oppose with might and main the tendency to this or that political and religious organization, or to games and athletic exercises, or to wealth and industrialism, and try violently to stop it. But the flexibility which sweetness and light give, and which is one of the rewards of culture pursued in good faith, enables a man to see that a tendency may be necessary, and even, as a preparation for something in the future, salutary, and yet that the generations or individuals who obey this tendency are sacrificed to it, that they fall short of the hope of perfection by following it; and that its mischiefs are to be criticized, lest it should take too firm a hold and last after it has served its purpose.

Mr. Gladstone well pointed out, in a speech at Paris,—and others have pointed out the same thing,—how necessary is the present great movement towards wealth and industrialism, in order to lay broad foundations of material well-being for the society of the future. The worst of these justifications is, that they are generally addressed to the very people engaged, body and soul, in the movement in question; at all events, that they are always seized with the greatest avidity by these people, and taken by them as quite justifying their life; and that thus they tend to harden them in their sins. Now, culture admits the necessity of the movement towards fortune-making and exaggerated industrialism, readily allows that the future may derive benefit from it; but insists, at the same time, that the passing generations of industrialists,—forming, for the most part, the stout main body of Philistinism,—are sacrificed to it. In the same way, the result of all the games and sports which occupy the passing generation of boys and young men may be the establishment of a better and sounder physical type for the future to work with. Culture does not set itself against the games and sports; it congratulates the future, and hopes it will make a good use of its improved physical basis; but it points out that our passing generation of boys and young men is, meantime, sacrificed. Puritanism was perhaps necessary to develop the moral fibre of the English race, Nonconformity to break the yoke of ecclesiastical domination over men's minds and to prepare the way for freedom of thought in the distant future; still, culture points out that the harmonious perfection of generations of Puritans and Nonconformists have been, in consequence, sacrificed. Freedom of speech may be necessary for the society of the future, but the young lions of the *Daily Telegraph* in the meanwhile are sacrificed. A voice for every man in his country's government may be necessary for the society of the future, but meanwhile Mr. Beales and Mr. Bradlaugh are sacrificed.

Oxford, the Oxford of the past, has many faults; and she has heavily paid for them in defeat, in isolation, in want of hold upon the modern world. Yet we in Oxford, brought up amidst the beauty and sweetness of that beautiful place, have not failed to seize one truth,—the truth that beauty and sweetness are essential characters of a complete human perfection. When I insist on this, I am all in the faith and tradition of Oxford. I say boldly that this our sentiment for beauty and sweetness, our sentiment against hideousness and rawness, has been at the bottom of our attachment to so many beaten causes, of our opposition to so many triumphant movements. And the sentiment is true, and has never been wholly defeated, and has shown its power even in its defeat. We have not won our political battles, we have not carried our main points, we have not stopped our adversaries' advance, we have not marched victoriously with the modern world; but we have told silently upon the mind of the country, we have prepared currents of feeling which sap our adversaries' position when it seems gained, we have kept up our own communications with the future. . . .

The pursuit of perfection, then is the pursuit of sweetness and light. He who works for sweetness and light, works to make reason and the will of God prevail. He who works for machinery, he who works for hatred, works only for confusion. Culture looks beyond machinery, culture hates hatred; culture has one great passion, the passion for sweetness and light. It has one even yet greater!—the passion for making them *prevail*. It is not satisfied till we *all* come to a perfect man; it knows that the sweetness and light of the few must be imperfect until the raw and unkindled masses of humanity are touched with sweetness and light. If I have not shrunk from saying that we must work for sweetness and light, so neither have I shrunk from saying that we must have a broad basis, must have sweetness and light for as many as possible. Again and again I have insisted how those are the happy moments of humanity, how those are the marking epochs of a people's life, how those are the flowering times for literature and art and all the creative power of genius, when there is a *national* glow of life and thought, when the whole of society is in the fullest measure permeated by thought, sensible to beauty, intelligent and alive. Only it must be *real* thought and *real* beauty; *real* sweetness and *real* light. Plenty of people will try to give the masses, as they call them, an intellectual food prepared and adapted in the way they think proper for the actual condition of the masses. The ordinary popular literature is an example of this way of working on the masses. Plenty of people will try to indoctrinate the masses with the set of ideas and judgments constituting the creed of their own profession or party. Our religious and political organizations give an example of this way of working on the masses. I condemn neither way; but culture works differently. It does not try to teach down to the level of inferior classes; it does not try to win them for this or that sect of its own, with ready-made judgments and watchwords. It seeks to do away with classes; to make the best that has been thought and known in the world current everywhere; to make all men live in an atmosphere of sweetness and light, where they may use ideas, as it uses them itself, freely,—nourished, and not bound by them.

This is the *social idea;* and the men of culture are the true apostles of equality. The great men of culture are those who have had a passion for diffusing, for making prevail, for carrying from one end of society to the other, the best knowledge, the best ideas of their time; who have laboured to divest knowledge of all that was harsh, uncouth, difficult, abstract, professional, exclusive; to humanize it, to make it efficient outside the clique of the cultivated and learned, yet still remaining the *best* knowledge and thought of the time, and a true source, therefore, of sweetness and light. Such a man was Abelard in the Middle Ages, in spite of all his imperfections; and thence the boundless emotion and enthusiasm which Abelard excited. Such were Lessing and Herder in Germany, at the end of the last century; and their services to Germany were in this way inestimably precious. Generations will pass, and literary monuments will accumulate, and works far more perfect than the works of Lessing and Herder will be produced in Germany; and yet the names of these two men will fill a German with a reverence and enthusiasm such as the names of the most gifted masters will hardly awaken. And why? Because they *humanized* knowledge; because they broadened the basis of life and intelligence; because they worked powerfully to diffuse sweetness and light, to make reason and the will of God prevail. With Saint Augustine they said: 'Let us not leave thee alone to make in the secret of thy knowledge, as thou didst before the creation of the firmament, the division of light from darkness; let the children of thy spirit, placed in their firmament, make their light shine upon the earth, mark the division of night and day, and announce the revolution of the times; for the old order is passed, and the new arises; the night is spent, the day is come forth; and thou shalt crown the year with thy blessing, when thou shalt send forth labourers into thy harvest sown by other hands than theirs; when thou shalt send forth new labourers to new seed-times, whereof the harvest shall be not yet.'

from *Culture and Anarchy*

More is not Better

... If, however, taking some other criterion of man's well-being than the cities he has built and the manufactures he has produced, we persist in thinking that our social progress would be happier if there were not so many of us so very poor, and in busying ourselves with notions of in some way or other adjusting the poor man and business one to the other, and not multiplying the one and the other mechanically and blindly, then our Liberal friends, the appointed doctors of free-trade, take us up very sharply. 'Art is long,' says the *Times*, 'and life is short; for the most part we settle things first and understand them afterwards. Let us have as few theories as possible; what is wanted is not the light of speculation. If nothing worked well of which the theory was not perfectly understood, we should be in sad confusion. The relations of labour and capital, we are told, are not understood, yet trade and commerce, on the whole, work satisfactorily.' I quote from the *Times* of only the other day. But thoughts like these, as I have often pointed out, are thoroughly British thoughts, and we have been familiar with them for years.

Or, if we want more of a philosophy of the matter than this, our free-trade friends have two axioms for us, axioms laid down by their justly esteemed doctors, which they think ought to satisfy us entirely. One is, that, other things being equal, the more population increases, the more does production increase to keep pace with it; because men by their numbers and contact call forth all manner of activities and resources in one another and in nature, which, when men are few and sparse, are never developed. The other is, that, although population always tends to equal the means of subsistence, yet people's notions of what subsistence is enlarge as civilization advances, and take in a number of things beyond the bare necessities of life; and thus, therefore, is supplied whatever check on population is needed. But the error of our friends is precisely, perhaps, that they apply axioms of this sort as if they were self-acting laws which will put themselves into operation without trouble or planning on our part, if we will only pursue free-trade, business, and population zealously and staunchly. Whereas the real truth is, that, however the case might be under other circumstances, yet in fact, as we now manage the matter, the enlarged conception of what is included in *subsistence* does not operate to prevent the bringing into the world of numbers of people who but just attain to the barest necessaries of life or who even fail to attain to them; while, again, though production may increase as population increases, yet it seems that the production may be of such a kind, and so related, or rather non-related, to population, that the population may be little the better for it.

For instance, with the increase of population since Queen Elizabeth's time the production of silk-stockings has wonderfully increased, and silk-stockings have become much cheaper, and procurable in greater abundance by many more people, and tend perhaps, as population and manufactures increase, to get cheaper and cheaper, and at last to become, according to Bastiat's favourite image, a common free property of the human race, like light and air. But bread and bacon have not become much cheaper with the increase of population since Queen Elizabeth's time, nor procurable in much greater abundance by many more people; neither do they seem at all to promise to become, like light and air, a common free property of the human race. And if bread and bacon have not kept pace with our population, and we have many more people in want of them now than in Queen Elizabeth's time, it seems vain to tell us that silk-stockings have kept pace with our population, or even more than kept pace with it, and that we are to get our comfort out of that.

In short, it turns out that our pursuit of free-trade, as of so many other things, has been too mechanical. We fix upon some subject, which in this case is the production of wealth, and the increase of manufactures, population, and commerce through free-trade as a kind of one thing needful, or end in itself; and then we pursue it staunchly and mechanically, and say that it is our duty to pursue it staunchly and mechanically, not to see how it is related to the whole intelligible law of things and to full human perfection, or to treat it as the piece of machinery, of varying value as its relations to the intelligible law of things vary, which it really is.

So it is of no use to say to the *Times*, and to our Liberal friends rejoicing in the possession of their talisman of free-trade, that about one in nineteen of our population is a pauper, and that, this being so, trade and commerce can hardly be said to prove by their satisfactory working that it matters nothing whether the relations between labour and capital are understood or not; nay, that we can hardly be said not to be in sad confusion. For here our faith in the staunch mechanical pursuit of a fixed object comes in, and covers itself with that imposing and colossal necessitarianism of the *Times* which we have before noticed. And this necessitarianism, taking for granted that an increase in trade and population is a good in itself, one of the chiefest of goods, tells us that disturbances of human happiness caused by ebbs and flows in the tide of trade and business, which, on the whole, steadily mounts, are inevitable and not to be quarrelled with. This firm philosophy I seek to call to mind when I am in the East of London, whither my avocations often lead me; and, indeed, to fortify myself against the depressing sights which on these occasions assail us, I have transcribed from the *Times* one strain of this kind, full of the finest economical doctrine, and always carry it about with me. The passage is this:

'The East End is the most commercial, the most industrial, the most fluctuating region of the metropolis. It is always the first to suffer; for it is the creature of prosperity, and falls to the ground the instant there is no wind to bear it up. The whole of that region is covered with huge docks, shipyards, manufactories, and a wilderness of small houses, all full of life and happiness in brisk times, but in dull times withered and lifeless, like the deserts we read of in the East. Now their brief spring is over. There is no one to blame for this; it is the result of Nature's simplest laws!' We must all agree that it is impossible that anything can be firmer than this, or show a surer faith in the working of free-trade, as our Liberal friends understand and employ it.

But, if we still at all doubt whether the indefinite multiplication of manufactories and small houses can be such an absolute good in itself as to counterbalance the indefinite multiplication of poor people, we shall learn that this multiplication of poor people, too, is an absolute good in itself, and the result of divine and beautiful laws. This is indeed a favourite thesis with our Philistine friends, and I have already noticed the pride and gratitude with which they receive certain articles in the *Times*, dilating to thankful and solemn language on the majestic growth of our population. But I prefer to quote now, on this topic, the words of an ingenious young Scotch writer, Mr. Robert Buchanan, because he invests with so much imagination and poetry this current idea of the blessed and even divine character which the multiplying of population is supposed in itself to have. 'We move to multiplicity,' says Mr. Robert Buchanan. 'If there is one quality which seems God's, and his exclusively, it seems that divine philoprogenitiveness, that passionate love of distribution and expansion into living forms. Every animal added seems a new ecstasy to the Maker; every life added, a new embodiment of his love. He would *swarm* the earth with beings. There are never enough. Life, life, life,—faces gleaming, hearts beating, must fill every cranny. Not a corner is suffered to remain empty. The whole earth breeds, and God glories.'

It is a little unjust, perhaps, to attribute to the Divinity exclusively this philoprogenitiveness, which the British Philistine, and the poorer class of Irish, may certainly claim to share with him; yet how inspiring is here the whole strain of thought! and these beautiful words, too, I carry about with me in the East of London, and often read them there. They are quite in agreement with the popular language one is accustomed to hear about children and large families, which describes children as *sent*. And a line of poetry, which Mr. Robert Buchanan throws in presently after the poetical prose I have quoted,—

'Tis the old story of the fig-leaf time—

this fine line, too, naturally connects itself, when one is in the East of London, with the idea of God's desire to *swarm* the earth with beings; because the swarming of the earth with beings does indeed, in the East of London, so seem to revive *the old story of the fig-leaf time*, such a number of the people one meets there having hardly a rag to cover them; and the more the swarming goes on, the more it promises to revive this old story. And when the story is perfectly revived, the swarming quite completed, and every cranny choke-full, then, too, no doubt, the faces in the

East of London will be gleaming faces, which Mr. Robert Buchanan says it is God's desire they should be, and which every one must perceive they are not at present, but, on the contrary, very miserable.

But to prevent all this philosophy and poetry from quite running away with us, and making us think with the *Times*, and our practical Liberal free-traders, and the British Philistines generally, that the increase of houses and manufactories, or the increase of population, are absolute goods in themselves, to be mechanically pursued, and to be worshipped like fetishes,—to prevent this, we have got that notion of ours immovably fixed, of which I have long ago spoken, the notion that culture, or the study of perfection, leads us to conceive of no perfection as being real which is not a *general* perfection, embracing all our fellow-men with whom we have to do. Such is the sympathy which binds humanity together, that we are, indeed, as our religion says, members of one body, and if one member suffer, all the members suffer with it. Individual perfection is impossible so long as the rest of mankind are not perfected along with us. 'The *multitude* of the wise is the welfare of the world,' says the wise man. And to this effect that excellent and often-quoted guide of ours, Bishop Wilson, has some striking words:—'It is not,' says he, 'so much our neighbour's interest as our own that we love him.' And again he says: 'Our salvation does in some measure depend upon that of others.' And the author of the *Imitation* puts the same thing admirably when he says:— '*Obscurior etiam via ad coelum videbatur quando tam pauci regnum coelorum quaerere curabant; the fewer there are who follow the way to perfection, the harder that way is to find.' So all our fellow-men, in the East of London and elsewhere, we must take along with us in the progress towards perfection, if we ourselves really, as we profess, want to be perfect; and we must not let the worship of any fetish, any machinery, such as manufactures or population,—which are not, like perfection, absolute goods in themselves, though we think them so,—create for us such a multitude of miserable, sunken, and ignorant human beings, that to carry them all along with us is impossible, and perforce they must for the most part be left by us in their degradation and wretchedness. But evidently the conception of free-trade, on which our Liberal friends vaunt themselves, and in which they think they have found the secret of national prosperity,—evidently, I say, the mere unfettered pursuit of the production of wealth, and the mere mechanical multiplying, for this end, of manufactures and population, threatens to create for us, if it has not created already, those vast, miserable, unmanageable masses of sunken people, to the existence of which we are, as we have seen, absolutely forbidden to reconcile ourselves, in spite of all that the philosophy of the *Times* and the poetry of Mr. Robert Buchanan may say to persuade us. . . .

I remember, only the other day, a good man looking with me upon a multitude of children who were gathered before us in one of the most miserable regions of London,—children eaten up with disease, half-sized, half-fed, half-clothed, neglected by their parents, without health, without home, without hope,— said to me: 'The one thing really needful is to teach these little ones to succour one another, if only with a cup of cold water; but now, from one end of the country to the other, one hears nothing but the cry for knowledge, knowledge, knowledge!' And yet surely, so long as these children are there in these festering masses, without health, without home, without hope, and so long as their multitude is perpetually swelling, charged with misery they must still be for themselves, charged with misery they must still be for us, whether they help one another with a cup of cold water or no; and the knowledge how to prevent their accumulating is necessary, even to give their moral life and growth a fair chance! . . .

Everything, in short, confirms us in the doctrine, so un-palatable to the believers in action, that our main business at the present moment is not so much to work away at certain crude reforms of which we have already the scheme in our own mind, as to create, through the help of that culture which at the very outset we began by praising and recommending, a frame of mind out of which the schemes of really fruitful reforms may with time grow. At any rate, we ourselves must put up with our friends' impatience, and with their reproaches against cultivated inaction, and must still decline to lend a hand to their practical operations, until we, for our own part, at least, have grown a little clearer about the nature of real good, and have arrived nearer to a condition of mind out of which really fruitful and solid operations may spring.

from 'Our Liberal Practitioners' in *Culture and Anarchy*

Lines Written on the Seashore at Eaglehurst, July 12, 1836

NAIADS were wont of old to dwell
Beneath the boundless Ocean's swell
And sport midst Halls of coral reared
Where winds and angry waters feared
To force their rushing way,
And crowned with sea-weed dance along
With bounding steps and mirth and song
While each perchance presided o'er
Some favour'd glen on wooded shore
    With mild and gentle sway.   10

What Naiad then—what Nymph presides
To shelter thee from winds and tides
To deck thy wooded cliff with flowers
To revel mid thy sea-girt bowers
    And haunts, O Eaglehurst?
If Thetis self had deigned to prove
For some sweet spot peculiar love
Sure thou wert worthy of her sway
Thus cradled in thy quiet Bay
    By woodland fairies nurst.   20

What though the murmur of the sea
Beats gently on the sandy lea
And ever restless fills the ear

With sounds which it is sweet to hear
    On many a quiet shore
Yet here it seems as if the wave
Were struggling with the sand to lave
The foot of yonder wooded cliff—
And then a barrier firm and stiff
    Opposed the Ocean's roar.   30

Still restlessly it struggles on
O'er sea-weed fair, o'er shell and stone
Although yon castled height looks down
And on the billows seems to frown
    And bid the Invader go.
But other scenes than castled towers,
The flowery fields, the woods and bowers
Invite the Intruder onward still
But while his Fancy takes its fill
    His waves must roll below.   40

FROM

Alaric at Rome

(How the calm of the city was shattered by invasion)

Hast thou not marked on a wild autumn day
When the wind slumbereth in a sudden lull,
What deathlike stillness o'er the landscape lay,
How calmly sad, how sadly beautiful;
How each bright tint of tree, and flower, and heath
Were mingling with the sere and withered hues of death.

And thus, beneath the clear, calm, vault of heaven
In mournful loveliness that city lay
And thus, amid the glorious hues of even
That city told of languor and decay: 10
    Till what at morning's hour lookt warm and bright
Was cold and sad beneath that breathless, voiceless night.

Soon was that stillness broken: like the cry
Of the hoarse onset of the surging wave,
Or louder rush of whirlwinds sweeping by
Was the wild shout those Gothic myriads gave,
    As towered on high, above their moonlit road,
Scenes where a Caesar triumpht, or a Scipio trod.

COMMENTARY

SHAKESPEARE, p. 25
This poem is discussed by F. R. Leavis in *Education and the University*, pp. 73–76.

THE FORSAKEN MERMAN, p. 25
Some readers see in this poem (the story of which Arnold took from a Danish folk tale) the tension between the poet's devotion to his admired father's Christianity and the attraction he felt for the vitality of paganism. Cf. Arnold's essay 'Pagan and Mediaeval Religious Sentiment': 'The poetry of later paganism lived by the senses and understanding; the poetry of mediaeval Christianity lived by the heart and imagination.'

CADMUS AND HARMONIA, p. 30
In the volume of his poems published in 1852 Arnold included 'Empedocles on Etna', a long poem about the philosopher, scientist, poet and statesman who lived *c.* 493–433 in Sicily. He omitted the work from his next collection of poems, except for the lines printed here.

Cadmus was the mythical founder of Thebes, who with his wife Harmonia fled to Illyria in their old age; there they were changed into serpents.

TO MARGUERITE, IN RETURNING A VOLUME OF THE LETTERS OF ORTIS, p. 32
Arnold's original title is given here; the book was a novel.

MEMORIAL VERSES, p. 33
Goethe died in 1832, Byron at Missolonghi (whither he had gone to help the insurgent Greeks) in 1824, and Wordsworth in 1850. The last-named was buried in Grasmere churchyard, near which the Rotha flows.

from SOHRAB AND RUSTUM, p. 42

In an extremely long note of his own Arnold gives a prose account of this story from Persian history. The extended similes markedly imitate those of Milton and especially Homer. The extracts given here start at *l.448* of the original.

l.13. *Afrasiab* was leader of the Tartar forces.

l.14. *Tartar:* the Tatars (their proper name) were a Mongol tribe that overran Eastern Europe in the thirteenth century. Among them were Turks and Cossacks.

l.15. *Oxus:* now the Amu Darya (in the Soviet Union), which flows from the Pamir Mountains to the Aral Sea.

l.195. When Sohrab's mother, Tehmineh, revealed to him the secret of his birth and told him to seek his father, she tattooed the Griffin on his arm.

l.232. *Jemshid:* an early legendary ruler of Persia and reputed inventor of the arts of medicine, ironwork and so on.

Persepolis, the ancient capital of Persia, was near the modern Shiraz.

l.251. i.e. northwards.

Orgunje: the modern Urgench in Uzbekistan.

PHILOMELA, p. 50

According to the Latin version of a Greek legend, Tereus, king of Thrace, was married to Procne. He seduced her sister Philomela, and then cut out her tongue to prevent her telling; but she wove a message to Procne. The latter killed her own and Tereus' child and served up the flesh for Tereus to eat. Finding this out, Tereus pursued the women, but Philomela was turned into a nightingale and Procne into a swallow.

THE SCHOLAR GIPSY, p. 52

Arnold took the story from *The Vanity of Dogmatizing* (1661) by Joseph Glanvil, Rector of Bath Abbey, and a believer in witchcraft and the pre-existence of souls. Arnold's note gives the quotation:

> There was very lately a lad in the University of Oxford, who was by his poverty forced to leave his studies there; and at last to join himself to a company of vagabond gipsies. Among these extravagant people, by the insinuating subtilty of his carriage, he quickly got so much of their love and esteem as that they discovered to him their mystery. After he had been a pretty while well exercised in the trade, there

chanced to ride by a couple of scholars, who had formerly been of his acquaintance. They quickly spied out their old friend among the gipsies; and he gave them an account of the necessity which drove him to that kind of life, and told them that the people he went with were not such imposters as they were taken for, but that they had a traditional kind of learning among them, and could do wonders by the power of imagination, their fancy binding that of others: that himself had learned much of their art, and when he had compassed the whole secret, he intended, he said, to leave their company, and give the world an account of what he had learned.

The source of the poem lay in the contrast between Arnold's feelings about the Oxfordshire countryside and the times he spent there with the companions of his youth, and the feelings stirred in him by much contact with an industrialized and commercialized England. Cf. J. D. Jump in the Pelican *Guide to English Literature*, Vol. 6, p. 310, and F. R. Leavis in *The Common Pursuit*, who writes: 'He offers the Scholar . . . as the symbol of a spiritual superiority . . . But . . . what the poem actually offers is a charm of relaxation, a holiday from serious aims and exacting business.' (pp. 29, 30).

l.69.   *Cumner (Cumnor) Hills:* about 4 m. south-west of Oxford.

l.73.   *Bab-lock-hithe* (Bablock Hythe): about 5 m. from Oxford, on the Isis or upper Thames, where there is a ferry.

l.91.   *Godstow Bridge:* On the upper Thames about 3 m. north-west of Oxford.

ll.182–190.   At various times these lines have been taken to refer to Goethe, Tennyson and Carlyle respectively.

ll.208, 209.   *Dido*, Queen of Carthage, entertained Aeneas on his way home from the siege of Troy, and killed herself when he deserted her.

l.232.   The Scholar is urged to escape the people of the present, as a quiet trader from Tyre (on the coast of what is now Lebanon) fled the noisy Greeks and escaped by way of the Syrtes (shallow straits between Sicily and N. Africa) to trade with the people of Spain.

THE 'DEATH' OF AEPYTUS, p. 60

These lines are taken from the long tragedy in verse that Arnold thought would be a fitting accompaniment to his becoming Professor of Poetry at Oxford.

This elegy (i.e. poem of reflective lament for the dead) throughout refers back to 'The Scholar Gipsy'. It is written in the pastoral mode, which started in Sicily and was followed at various times in most of the literatures of Europe. Its characteristic is to achieve simplicity of thought and action by writing about real people as if they were rustics. See note below on *l.*84.

*l.*2. The Hinkseys are on the outskirts of Oxford.

*l.*4. I.e. there is a new inn-keeper.

*l.*10. *Thyrsis;* see note below on *l.*80.

*l.*80. Corydon and Thyrsis contend against one another in song, in a poem by Virgil; Thyrsis is defeated. Arnold calls Clough 'Thyrsis' because they had been friendly rivals.

*l.*84. *Bion,* who flourished *c.* 100 B.C. in Sicily, was one of the pastoral poets from whom derived the convention of writing about people as if they were shepherds.

*ll.*86–88. *Pluto* carried away *Persephone* (Proserpina was a Roman mispronunciation of the Greek name) to be his queen in the underworld.

*l.*90. *Orpheus* was the mythical poet who followed his dead wife to the underworld and won her back by charming the guardians of the place with his lyre.

*l.*95. *Enna:* the vale in Sicily where Persephone was gathering flowers when carried off by Pluto.

*l.*109. *Ensham* (Eynsham) is about 6 m. north-west of Oxford.

*l.*123. *Wytham* is immediately north-west of Oxford.

*l.*167. *Florence* is on the river Arno.

*l.*177. Persephone's mother was Demeter.

*ll.*181–191. Arnold has merged two legends. Daphnis, a Greek shepherd, was blinded by a nymph whose love he would not return. His sight was later restored. Another Daphnis was rescued from Lityerses, a Phrygian king, who made all travellers compete with him at reaping, and killed the losers. The 'Lityerses-song' was sung by corn-reapers.

SAINT BRANDAN, p. 69

The saint founded several monasteries, including the Benedictine community at Clonfert in Ireland, in the sixth century. He was fond of sailing and there are some improbable stories of his adventures. Cf.

S. Baring-Gould and John Fisher, *The Lives of the British Saints* (London 1907–13).

DOVER BEACH, p. 72

J. D. Jump (Pelican *Guide to English Literature*, Vol. 6, p. 310) believes this to be Arnold's only great poem. Before examining it closely, he comments:

> 'Dover Beach' is entirely free from . . . poeticality. It is a short poem, but it embraces a great range and depth of significance. As elsewhere, Arnold discloses his melancholy preoccupation with the thought of the inevitable decline of religious faith; and he expresses the belief that in a successful love-relationship he may realize values to which 'the world' is hostile. But he does not merely ruminate upon these ideas. He conveys them to us more by the 'moon-blanch'd' landscape which he creates than by his direct statement of them.

PALLADIUM, p. 73

This was the ancient sacred image of Pallas Athene. It was believed that while it was kept safe in Troy the city would not fall to the besieging Greeks. Troy (modern name Hissarlik) lies near the western entrance to the Dardanelles, on the triangular plateau between the rivers Scamander (Xanthus) and Simois.

The notion of the soul retiring from the battle of life is characteristically Arnoldian. Here he dignifies the pose by associating it with an idealized Classical past.

THE LAST WORD, p. 76

When this poem was written (1865–1867), Arnold was turning over in his mind the thoughts about the movements and characters of his day that took shape first in the essay 'Democracy' and later in *Culture and Anarchy*. The poem suggests that Arnold had other feelings than the ironical buoyancy and cheerfulness that characterize so much of the book.

STANZAS FROM THE GRANDE CHARTREUSE, p. 83

The first 108 lines of the 'Stanzas' are given here.

In 1084 St Bruno founded the Carthusian order of monks at the Grande Chartreuse, near Grenoble. They wear white habits, observe silence, and live each in a separate small dwelling within the monastery, though meeting for services.

ROME-SICKNESS, p. 87
As Arnold walks in the Surrey countryside he thinks of places endeared
to him, first Switzerland, and then Italy. Frascati is a holiday resort 12 m.
south-east of Rome, in the Alban Hills.

S.S. 'LUSITANIA', p. 88
The poem reflects Arnold's anxiety, for he had lost two of his sons
when the third sailed to Australia. The places mentioned, first in the
quotation from Dante (the voice of Ulysses is relating the events that
led up to his death) and then in *ll*.11 and 14, show that though the
Suez Canal had been open for some years the steamer track taken by
the *Lusitania* went round by Spain, the Canaries (where rises the Peak
of Tenerife) and West Africa.

EXAMINATIONS (2), p. 95
A letter to the *Pall Mall Gazette* of 5th October 1870, signed 'M.A.'
(as were many of his private letters), seems almost certainly by Arnold,
and makes a strong case against the spread of examinations.

THE STANDARD OF LIFE, p. 96
'Canst thou not minister . . .' see Macbeth, V iii.

DEMOCRACY, p. 98
This is part of the essay which Arnold added to his 1860 Report on
education on the Continent. The views expressed here were developed
in *Culture and Anarchy*; they show how his educational thought and
criticism grew from his professional duties.

THE FUNCTION OF CRITICISM, p. 105
The complete article acts as an introduction to *Essays in Criticism*,
first series, 1865, the volume which includes 'Heinrich Heine' and 'On
Translating Homer'.
Lord Somers (p. 110) presided over the drafting of the Declaration of
Rights on the abdication of James II.
Martin Luther (p. 111) was the German religious Reformer, 1483–1546.
Jacques Bossuet (p. 111) was the rigidly dogmatic French theologian,
1627–1704.

ON TRANSLATING HOMER, p. 115

The extract given here is part of a lecture Arnold delivered at Oxford, as Professor of Poetry. It is a good example of criticism based on the close reading of a text. Within a year of the appearance of the lectures in book form four new versions of the Iliad were published in England.

F. W. Newman's translation of the Iliad in 'unrhymed English metre' was published in 1856.

Pope's six volumes of the Iliad appeared in 1715-1720, after which, with assistance, he translated the Odyssey. The two greatly enriched him and he was able to buy the lease of the house at Twickenham where he lived for the rest of his life.

THE STUDY OF POETRY, p. 119

This essay was first published in 1880 as a general introduction to a four-volume anthology of the English poets from Chaucer to Rossetti, edited by T. H. Ward.

The three quotations from Milton on pp. 120, 121 come respectively from *Paradise Lost*, Bk. I, *l.*559; Bk. I, *l.*109; and Bk. IV, *l.*271.

POETRY AND LIFE, p. 123

The extract comes from Arnold's preface to the selection from the poet that he edited in 1879. Arnold's family used to go for holidays to the Lake District, and thus as a young man he came to know and admire Wordsworth in his old age.

Voltaire (p. 123) was the French philosopher, 1694-1778.
Lessing (p. 127) was the German critic and dramatic poet, 1729-1781.
Schiller (p. 127) was the German dramatist and poet, 1759-1805.
Leslie Stephen (p. 127), one of the soundest literary critics of the nineteenth century, lived from 1832 to 1904. Virginia Woolf was his daughter.

SWEETNESS AND LIGHT, p. 128

This extract forms the greater part of the first chapter of *Culture and Anarchy*, which was first published in 1869, just before a new government took office in February.

Bishop Wilson (p. 128) was an eighteenth-century divine, of Sodor and Man, and the author of *Maxims*.

John Bright (p. 132) was a Quaker radical politician.

Frederic Harrison was a young barrister and a warm supporter of working-class causes.

J. A. Roebuck (p. 133), M.P. for Sheffield, was a disciple and friend of John Stuart Mill. Roebuck was a radical, whose career was marked by his independence and vehemence in speech.

Benjamin Franklin (p. 136) was the American statesman and philosopher, who lived in Britain for eighteen years and then helped to frame the Constitution of the U.S.A.

Prof. T. H. Huxley (p. 140), scientist and distinguished supporter of Charles Darwin's theory of evolution, was a close friend of Arnold's, with whom he engaged in good-natured controversy. See p. 221 of the Dover Wilson edition of *Culture and Anarchy*.

'publice egestas . . .' (p. 140) means approximately 'Poverty in public, wealth in private'. Cf. J. K. Galbraith, *The Affluent Society*, especially Chapters 18 and 22.

Daily Telegraph (p. 140), founded in 1855 as the first penny newspaper, then occupied the place to fill which nowadays the chief contenders might be the *Daily Mirror* and the *Daily Express*.

Edmund Beales (p. 142) became president of the Reform League, and led one of the processions that in July 1866 broke down the railings of Hyde Park in order to hold a meeting there.

Charles Bradlaugh (p. 142), a member of the Reform League, was active for the reform of Parliament in 1866-67, and was present at the Hyde Park 'Riots'. Elected an M.P., he was at first refused admission on the ground that he would not take the oath on Scripture.

MORE IS NOT BETTER, p. 145

This comes from the last main essay in *Culture and Anarchy*, which was very much directed at the politicians of the time.

R. W. Buchanan (p. 149) was a Scottish novelist and journalist, who came to London about 1860, made a name as a poet, and attacked the pre-Raphaelite poets.

Imitation (p. 150), i.e. *De Imitatione Christi*, attributed to Thomas à Kempis, a fifteenth-century Augustinian monk; it was translated into English almost as soon as it appeared.

LINES WRITTEN ON THE SEASHORE AT EAGLEHURST, p. 152

Arnold wrote this poem at the age of thirteen, when on holiday at a country house on Southampton Water, belonging to a relative-by-marriage of his father's.

l.1. *Naiads* in classical mythology were the nymphs who personified lakes and rivers.

l.16. *Thetis:* a sea deity and mother of Achilles.

from ALARIC AT ROME, p. 154
These lines come from the prize poem of 228 lines which was recited at Rugby School on 12 June 1840.

Alaric (376–410) led the Visigoths against the Romans, and took Rome in 410.

INDEX OF TITLES AND FIRST LINES OF POEMS

INDEX OF TITLES AND TOPICS OF PROSE